£12·95p

COMMEDIA DELL'ARTE

COMMEDIA DELL'ARTE
at the COVRT of Louis XIV
a soft sculpture Representation
by PETER·A·BVCKNELL

STAINER & BELL : LONDON

Typeset by Pierson LeVesley Ltd
Printed and bound in Great Britain by Sackville Press Billericay Ltd

Produced by Editorial and Production Services Ltd, London

ISBN 0 85249 575 7

To
'Hilly'
and
Denise and Alain Guigère

CONTENTS

Acknowledgements and Bibliography	vi
Commedia dell'Arte	1
Making the Sculptures	4
Materials and Equipment	4
Order and Method	5
The Figures	
Molière	8
Arlequin	14
Brighella	20
Pantalone	26
Le Médecin	32
La Bien-Aimée	38
L'Amant	44
Columbine	50
Le Capitaine	56
Giangurgolo	62
Scaramouche	68
Pulcinella	74
Polichinelle	80
Crispin	86
Tartaglia	92
Pierrot	98
Mezzetino	104
Trivellino	110
Louis XIV	116

ACKNOWLEDGEMENTS

I am deeply grateful to the following for their assistance in completing this book and making the figures:

Jeremy Finlay for all the colour photographs accompanying the text,
Sheila Donaldson Walters for all the calligraphy accompanying the patterns,
Alain Guigère for making the chairs and the throne,
Oliver Mullett for typing the manuscript,
and to many of my good friends who gave so generously much of the materials, feathers, jewels, braids, lace, buttons, and so on, which started off the collection.

I would also particularly like to pay respect to the following authors in clarifying some of my own research and personal knowledge of Commedia dell'Arte:

Pierre Louis Duchartre, *The Italian Comedy* translated from the French by
    Randolph T. Weaver (Dover Publications, New York),
Giacomo Oreglia, *The Commedia dell'Arte*, translated by Lovett F. Edwards (Methuen),
Allardyce Nicoll, *World Drama* (Harrap),
Actors on Acting, edited with introductions and biographical notes by Toby Cole and
    Helen Krich Chinoy (Crown Publishers, New York).

Peter A. Bucknell

BOOKS ON CUTTING, MAKING, AND HISTORY OF COSTUME

Needle and Thread by Gisela Hein (Batsford)
Batsford book on sewing by Ann Ladbury (Batsford)
The Evolution of Fashion: Pattern and Cut 1066-1930 by Margot Hamilton Hill and
    Peter A. Bucknell (Batsford)
The Cut of Men's Clothes 1600-1900 by N. Waugh (Faber and Faber)

COMMEDIA DELL'ARTE

ORIGINS AND DEVELOPMENT

However obscure the origins, improvised playing of comedies and home-spun stories clearly goes back to the early beginnings of man's history. It is known that the Commedia's formative years were in Italy early in the sixteenth century, performed by professional players and not, as most earlier plays had been, by members of the Church, scholars or amateurs. The actors of Commedia set out to amuse, to entertain, moving from town to town, village to village and gaining such popularity that from the middle of the sixteenth century their performances were demanded in all the major countries of Europe. They stayed in demand for over two hundred years.

Their art was flagrantly theatrical, a combination of speech and voice, movement, music, song, dance, mime, and visual display; its basis was improvisation. They had some things in common with the ancient *Phylakes* or 'gossip players' of southern Italy (*c.* 400 BC), who travelled to Greece and were no doubt later influenced by the written comedies of Aristophanes and Menander. The themes of the Greek stories were based on burlesques of contemporary situations or 'sent-up' stories of the gods and goddesses. They were crude, obscene and grotesque, as can be seen from the numerous Greek vases decorated with scenes recording their performances. All the characters wore caricature masks, and deformed their bodies with padding, many wearing the leather phallus. Their stage was a simple collapsible platform backed by modest pieces of scenery.

The improvised Atellan farces which also came from southern Italy, probably in the fourth century BC, were first played by amateurs; but by the third century BC professional companies toured the countryside playing anywhere they could put up their stage (and, on occasion, in theatres). Only a few names of the farces and a list of the stock characters are extant: Pappus (perhaps an early Pantalone), Doxenus or Dossennus (a cunning hunchbacked slave), Bucco (a stupid swaggering oaf) and Maccus (a sensual coward). These troupes included not only actors but acrobats and 'funny acts'; and their costumes and masks were very similar to those worn by the *Phylakes* players. No doubt they influenced the written comedies of Plautus, and even the more elegant comedies of Terence who included in his plays a mass of love affairs and intrigues between gallant young gentlemen and charming young ladies. As with the scenarios of the Commedia the central theme was always love.

The Atellan farces suffered after the fall of Rome, and also from the attacks of the Church on actors in general. To escape persecution, the players travelled further afield to northern Europe (establishing the strolling players, maskers and mummers), and most probably migrated to the Near East, particularly Byzantium. At the fall of Constantinople (Byzantium) in 1453, new generations of actors, originally of Italian stock but who had travelled the world, returned to Italy, and it is just possible that similarities between Commedia dell'Arte and aspects of puppet shows in Turkey, India, Japan and Java are not coincidence, as for example in the character of Punch (Polichinelle) and the costume of Pantalone.

The sixteenth-century companies included both men and women (women playing important roles for the first time in theatre history), appearing at fairs, markets, and sometimes before the great families in their halls. They included not only the actors but also acrobats, tumblers, musicians, dancers, and even performing animals. There was no written text, only a simple scenario outlining the plot. Their freedom of speech spared no one (no matter who might be in the audience) from comments on individuals or criticism and mockery of the authorities and local dignitaries. Hence they were always in fear of excommunication from the Church or eviction by the establishment. They did not seem to care!

As the century progressed they became highly organised and disciplined, and their art and technique was firmly established by the character types (with their names and special costumes), the scenarios and the manner of performance. In the seventeenth century their art was known at almost every European court, and some companies were provided with semi-permanent homes, theatres, architects, designers of scenery and, of course, court patronage. Playwrights at court theatres were bound to be influenced by the unique, gay abandon and spontaneity of mime and speech in the Commedia. Scenes in Shakespeare, Molière, and in plays as late as those of Gozzi and Marivaux in the first half of the eighteenth century acknowledge this.

The Commedia was a popular theatre enjoyed by all, nowhere more so than in France, where Louis XIV gave them their own theatre and his patronage. In Paris they became known as the Comédie-Italienne to distinguish them from the Comédie-Francaise, though they incorporated French into their native language as a gesture to their hosts. As their forebears did, the Paris companies continually risked causing offence with their parodies of court happenings and political scandal. In 1697 they went too far even for the Sun King, and were deported. Returning to Paris after the King's death in 1716, they re-established themselves for a time; but with the suppression of improvised playing and the taking over of many roles by French actors using the French language, scenarios (and dialogue) became scripted. Thus the uniqueness of their art was destroyed. The Parisian audiences came to consider the Commedia no longer fashionable, and by 1801 the Comédie-Italienne amalgamated with another company to be known as the Opéra Comique. Losing their name they soon ceased to exist, deteriorating into Harlequinades and 'Punch and Judy' puppet shows.

Today, or not so very long ago, reflections of their joyous entertainment could be seen in the English Christmas Pantomime (originally containing a Harlequinade), with its spectacle, popular songs and music, ballets, variety acts, well-known 'celebrity' comedians, and, of course, a good, strong and well-known story-line – the scenario.

The scenarios of the Commedia dell'Arte were brief, a guideline of action for the actors to interpret the plot; there was no playwright or producer to monitor what happened and therefore no two performances were ever exactly alike, although the actors and the head of the company (the *maestro*) would agree on the basic interpretation beforehand. No rehearsal was necessary. All the members of the company knew their allocated tasks and the actors their stock characters (and the limitations and freedom they were permitted within the scenario, which was posted in the wings of the theatre on the day of the performance). Usually a meeting was held, when all the members discussed the scenario, perhaps suggesting a new piece of stage business or a newly-prepared speech or soliloquy, or a song or dance, and agreeing a general basic timing for each sequence of the plot. A rough plan, mutually agreed, was all that was necessary. A dress rehearsal would have ruined the essence of their art – to improvise and seize upon a situation spontaneously, presenting it directly to the audience. The technique was based upon an ensemble, controlled by years of rigid discipline and individual perfection from the actors in the roles they played. Well over 1000 scenarios still exist, but they should not be considered 'literary' works.

The central theme was Love. The scenario outlined the plot, divided into acts, and the entrances and exits. Situations within each scene were defined, always with the list of characters. Scene-changes and the required stage properties were also listed. The performers were permitted to introduce into their various scenes stage 'business' called *lazzi*, as long as they returned to the story-line with a proper cue. A solo comic might talk directly to the audience or tell jokes about other characters in the play or even about local gossip. *Lazzi* could also introduce dances, disguises, songs and clowning. Some idea of what it may have been like can be seen today during a circus, when a group of clowns may make their arrival in a caricature of a car which explodes, falls to pieces, then miraculously functions again to take them out of the ring and allow the performance to continue. A later 'break' by the clowns might end, for no particular reason, by their all producing instruments and playing a 'pop' tune. Marcel Marceau's mimetic gifts echo the *lazzi* as he chases an imaginary bumble-bee or is caged in a box described only by the movements of his body. Some examples of *lazzi* found in surviving Commedia scenarios include:

A Harlequin who arrives on an eagle from above, in a Sedan-chair, or on a donkey.

An elaborate stone fountain which is discovered in full play: a gust of wind blows away the lightly-constructed piece of scenery revealing a group of characters spewing out water from their mouths or using watering cans. (No doubt in the early scenarios other 'watering holes' were used!)

A young girl who is alone in a garden surrounded by stone statues: suddenly one of the statues sneezes and they all descend from their plinths – actors dressed and painted in white.

A Pantalone who is persuaded that his breath smells badly and that some of his teeth should be removed: Harlequin arrives in the disguise of a doctor and with blacksmith's tools extracts Pantalone's teeth. (Echoes of our circus clowns again.)

Between the acts interludes were played, called 'entr'actes' or 'intermezzi', which could include transformation scenes, firework displays, acrobats, tumblers, performing animals, magicians, songs and solo dances or ballets – what we now think of as 'Variety'. Single members of the troupe in character sometimes performed their special acts in the intermezzo, such as:

Harlequin (acrobatics and tumbling)
Mezzetino (a song)
Pulcinella (walking the slackwire or performing on the trapeze)
Crispin (alone, not sure where he is, or how to fill the time –
    a 'classic' for stand-up comedians in any age)
Scaramouche (conjuring or mime)

The popularity of the various performers and their acts rose and fell according to the fashion of the day, and also to the uniqueness of a particular actor whose gifts could not be imi-

tated, like the great Fiorilli's Scaramouche or Poisson's Crispin in the Paris companies. Such 'star' actors came from all social classes – some very religious, others very cultured, including writers and composers. They played the same role for the whole of their working lives, frequently passing on their technique and characterisation for their sons or daughters to develop and make their own. There was a limited number of actors in each company. The major roles never varied, but many minor roles were from time to time introduced into the scenarios, appearing and disappearing from the comedies according to popularity. Some actors – the real stars – changed the name of their character, but the well-known established roles remained. A company usually had an ensemble of actors to play these established roles:

One or two sets of young lovers.

Two old men: the first, Pantalone, and the second, the Doctor.

The *zanni* (male servants and valets): the first, Brighella, and the second, Harlequin. There were many other servant/valet types, including Fiorilli's Scaramouche, Pierrot and Mezzetino, but Harlequin and Brighella always dominate the story-line in the scenario. Each had different characteristics, each had a special costume and make-up or mask, and each had a particular function and limitation within the scenario. Some were very bizarre and theatrical in their dress and behaviour, others were enchanting and elegant, but all were mischievous.

The *zagne* (female servants): they intrigued with the male servants and were usually dressed according to the fashion of the day. They did not wear the mask but were chosen for their mischievousness and charm. Many had little to do other than dance and sing or accompany the senior maids who played an active part in the comedy. The most well-known maid was Columbine.

The military: again there were many, some with more important roles than others. Like the servants, they all had their own particular characteristics, dress, and part to play in the comedy. The soldier types could include the Spanish, Italian or French Captain, Polichinelle (a French invention), Giangurgolo, and perhaps Crispin (another French invention), amongst many others.

Pulcinella: the odd man out, an enigmatic character who often changed his profession and performance according to the scenario.

As can be seen, all the roles were highly individualistic, each character having his or her own particular characterisation, speech and voice, movement, accomplishments, costume and mask. Therefore each was immediately recognisable by the audience on his or her entrance.

Originally all save the lovers wore the mask, which covered the entire face. This mask did not have a set expression, but was undefinable and provoking. Made out of soft leather, the expression could change with the facial contortions of the wearer. An entirely different technique in acting is required when wearing a mask, for all body movements and behaviour must conform to its expression and characterisation. Sometime during the sixteenth century, the mask became divided into two sections, one half covering the upper part of the face and the other section the lower jaw. Actors began to play discarding the lower section; some wore only a false nose; and during the second half of the seventeenth century certain characters discarded the mask altogether, resorting to make-up. Masked actors were not actors as some now define 'acting', in the sense of realism and 'being natural'. They were fantastic, supernatural, and bizarre – but very 'real' to their audiences.

In their formative years as strolling players, the Commedia

companies simply set up a collapsible platform backed with a curtain depicting a street scene, with perhaps two folding screens on either side representing special houses (Pantalone's for example) for entrances. These provided two entrances from the house doors and two in front of the backcloth. This scene would normally have been hidden by a curtain which opened after the 'Prologue' (spoken by a comedian having nothing to do with the scenario). Sometimes a second platform built on the stage made possible 'a play within a play'. Soon they resorted to scene changes, which became very fashionable in Italy during the Renaissance of classical thought and culture. These involved different back-drops, side wings, and elaborate stage properties – modest versions of the extravagant scene-changing and design of the court masques and operas, even including trapdoors and 'flying' apparatus. Once established in the courts of Europe, lucky companies had their own designer of stage settings and scene changes, working in a roofed theatre. The French company imported from Italy some of the greatest designers of the day to create these spectacles, which could include transformation scenes and very elaborate mechanical stage properties, with scene following scene in rapidity. A forest followed by a stormy sea and a shipwreck, then a temple, an orchard, a street or a city, a palace, hell, a garden: such a succession was not impossible for the seventeenth-century designer. The nearest we can come to it in today's theatre is in ballets like *The Sleeping Beauty*, *Cinderella* and *Casse-noisette*, or the constant scene-changes and staging effects in *The Magic Flute*. The endless possibilities of film superimpositions have perhaps taken their place.

MAKING THE SCULPTURES

MATERIALS AND EQUIPMENT

The Patterns

(a) All the patterns are to scale, usually half-scale of the original figures.

(b) In a few instances, the scale is reduced to one-quarter or one-eighth. Where this is so, it is clearly marked on the pattern.

(c) The maker can use the size of the patterns as shown, or, which is easier and preferable, scale up the patterns to any size.

(d) Although the patterns are accurate and correct in relation to the existing figures, the maker, when selecting from his or her own research and choice of visual information to interpret, should freely adapt the existing patterns and use them only as a guide. (From experience, in the making of several Harlequins, no one figure looks exactly like another when completed.)

(e) The basic figure is in each case based on two simple patterns: one for the face, body and legs, and feet (for front and back alike); and the second for the back and front of arms and hands. The design is based on the simple rag doll.

(f) No pattern gives seam, turning or hem allowances.

(g) If the maker has little or no experience in making sewn figures, it is advisable to leave good seams, turnings and hems to give leeway for minor alterations or adjustments due to stretch or thickness of material chosen.

(h) Do *not* cut any remaining patterns until you have made the basic figure. Then check pattern measurements with your basic figure, adjusting if necessary for variations caused by padding or materials used.

(i) Notes on the patterns describing the various parts have been kept to a minimum. For example, the notes on the patterns, in most instances, do not give linings, which should always be cut on the same grain as the top surface. A few very small patterns omit the name or number of pieces required (like the ears and face features). Where this occurs refer to the text or the sketches accompanying the patterns.

(j) Always test the size of the hat in relation to the padded head. In some instances you may find that the size of the head-measurement of the hat may need to be cut bigger or smaller according to the amount of padding placed in the head, the thickness of the hair, or the material chosen.

The Materials

(a) The sections in the book related to materials required are again only a guide, as many of the materials employed in the making of the originals were collected from friends. They were old, and in many instances antique, scraps of cloth of all descriptions no longer obtainable in haberdashers or fabric stores. In a few instances modern fabrics and materials like Lurex, brushed nylon and brushed cotton prove very useful substitutes, though it is much more amusing and exciting to beg, borrow or purloin from your friends old pieces of cloth, which always have a more beautiful quality: pure jap silk, brocades, lace, braids and ribbons, ring velvet, ottoman silk, watered silk, feathers, beads, pieces of jewellery, antique buttons – many never otherwise to be used again.

(b) Before commencing actual making collect as many different pieces of material and ornamentation as possible of all colours, weights, and textures, bearing in mind the traditional colours of many of the characters.

Colour is important for the balancing of tones and the range of colours required for each of the characters. This will be seen clearly when making the figure of Pantalone, who is basically all in reds, but in this medium the tones of red must vary to make the figure look well.

Texture is important – shiny, dull, rough, soft or smooth – again where the character is basically in one colour; for example the textures must vary in Scaramouche and the Doctor, who are both basically dressed from head to foot in black.

Weight is extremely important, as the scaled-down clothes must appear to hang correctly in proportion to the figure. In particular this should be borne in mind when making robes and coats, cloaks, skirts, and neck-frills and cuffs. Thicker materials are excellent for the basic body and arms.

(c) Great care should be taken in the choice of fabric for the faces and/or masks. Here is the centre of characterisation, and the fabric must be strong but capable of being stretched when padded to emphasise cheeks, chins, noses, beards etc.

(d) For padding you will need kapok for heads, soft cottonwool for thumbs and small features (noses), and fish or bird grit for feet and the lower parts of legs and hands. The rest of the padding can use up any old material.

(e) Do not commence any work until you have collected sufficient materials, grouping them together in the right colours, textures and weights for each character. Put the bundles into separate plastic bags with the name of the character fastened to the top.

Equipment

Needle and thread (thread of all colours)
Curved upholstery needle
Sewing machine
Scissors
Small sharp knife
Iron and ironing-board
Dyes, water-colours or poster paint
Finely-pointed number two sable brush
Colour felt pens of various thicknesses
Textile glues
Instantaneous epoxy glues
A rod rounded at one end or a wooden household spoon, and a chopstick.

Stitches

Sewing machine (but used with discretion)

Back-stitching (for most of the sewing)

Hand hemming

Very close oversewing, similar to that used in patchwork

Slip-stitching (sewing two pieces of fabric together on the right side without allowing the stitches to show).

A simple book on dressmaking will acquaint the maker with these stitches in diagram form but most home dressmakers will recognise them immediately. In all cases the stitches should be firm and strong, particularly the basic body, head and arms, which will have to stand the strain of vigorous and tightly-packed padding.

The detailed sections on making the figures which follow are written from experience during the two years of making the collection. On reflection, a few minor alterations have been made, but basically the process is the same. Essentials are patience, a reasonable skill in using a needle, imagination and ingenuity. The chosen objects asked for some elaborate and detailed work but equally interesting results can be achieved by simplifying details so as to aim at a more abstract and economic interpretation. In this collection, to quote some simplifications, the fingers are not separated or even drawn in, nor do the shoes have heels, as this was alien to the medium used. I did attempt to embroider the face features rather than resort to appliqué and painting with a fine sable brush, but the embroidered expression (a smile or a sneer) lost much of its vigour in contrast to the sweep of a brush or felt pen.

ORDER AND METHOD

The Basic Figure

All the figures should be made concurrently and completed to the same stage before commencing the next step, as no one character should take full attention at the expense of another. The aim is for an ensemble and not individual characters (though of course it is not necessary to follow this process if the maker wishes to make only one figure). The 'basic figure' incorporates parts of the costume like bodices, doublets, breeches, and in all instances stockings and shoes. In general, sew up all the front sections, starting from the head down to the feet, and do the same with the back. Many of the figures have quite a lot of braid-work and decoration applied to sections *before* sewing them together, as it is sometimes very difficult to apply decoration once the figure has been padded. When both back and front are completed place front to back with the wrong sides outermost, sew around the entire figure leaving a three or four inch gap about the chest level, turn right side out, and pad. The arms and hands are made up in exactly the same way. Your discretion is required when sewing them firmly to the shoulder of the body: only an inch or so for dangling arms, or much further down both back and front to angle them to the appropriate gesture.

Usually it is advisable not to sew the arms to the body until the body has been fully decorated and dressed. This also applies to the arms themselves, where it is advisable to add all decoration, cuffs and arm frills, etc. before sewing the arms in position.

Padding

Apart from the special requirements already listed under 'Materials', most of the padding used can be made of any cloth you can lay your hands on – socks, old sheets, nylon tights, old clothes, plastic bags – but it is essential to cut it into pieces no larger than one inch square. If you are attempting a large collection you will need quantities. I kept mine in three large black disposable plastic bags, adding all the time to keep them full.

The way the figure is padded must be left to the imagination of the maker, to give it the correct characterisation; for some characters the legs need to be very firm and vigorous, and for others supple so that there is more mobility at the knee joint. This is equally true when packing the arms.

The most successful method of padding is to start with the feet up to about knee level, padding with grit. Then continue padding with the pieces of cut-up cloth, always ramming it home with the wooden rod, until reaching the waistline. Then pad the head *very* firmly with kapok down as far as the neck and shoulders will be revealed when the figure is completed. A thin twelve-inch dowel rod should now be inserted, pushing it into the middle area of the padding of the head, to the centre of the neck, and through as far as it will go into the body. The dowel rod should then be angled to help characterisation of set of head to neck and shoulders. Finally pack as many pieces of the cut-up cloth as can be forced into the figure, particularly round the pelvis (padding is inclined to drop in time and the pelvis area, if padded very firmly, will keep the upper body padding in good position). Sew up the gap left in the side seam for padding, and the entire body of the figure is complete.

The arms and the hands are treated in a similar manner, beginning with grit or soft cottonwool until the filling reaches to just above the wrists. If using soft cottonwool, the narrow end of a chopstick is ideal to pad the thumb. The rest of the arms are padded with cut-up pieces of cloth. Lastly, sew up the gap left in the side seams for padding, and the arms are complete.

Remember to check measurements with your basic figure before cutting any more patterns (see above).

Additional Parts

The next process is to make and sew to the figure the skirts, belts, extra braiding and decoration, tunics, capes and mantles, over-robes, ruffs and collars, breeches etc. For some of this sewing the curved upholstery needle comes in handy. Cloaks and over-robes need to be lightly oversewn or caught on either side of the shoulder-line to keep them from slipping or shifting. After sewing on the arms the figure should now be complete save for the hair, head, hats and accessories.

All the hair is made from cotton *or* silk upholstery fringe unravelled to make it curl (and less bulky) *or* – which is much more adaptable – jute looped and stuck onto narrow strips of felt of the same colour. The lower edges of the loops are cut and unravelled to form curls or straightened out (depending on the character). For tighter curls, apply hair lacquer. The sections of hair are then placed carefully on the head (see below) and either sewn or glued in position. Where the figure is not wearing a hat, simply glue the jute to the head, following the hair-style. Lastly, trim and if appropriate thin out the hair to the required fashion. Some sewing may be needed to secure the finished style. Louis XIV wears a wig, therefore the final effect needs to look more formal. This is achieved by cutting the basic three shapes of the wig (two sides and the back) in felt, and glueing as many loops of the unravelled jute to the pieces as is possible, making sure that the result is rich and heavy in character and that the felt base is well and truly hidden by the projecting loops. Glue the three pieces to the sides and back of the head, add a fringe to the forehead and the wig is complete.

Head patterns are cut following two methods, depending on the character. These are either frontal, without protruding features; or in profile, giving the head its nose, beard etc. Where three dimensions are required, ears, nose and beard are added to the face. First sew the ears, with an interlining of thin card or felt, to either side of the head; then nose, padded with soft cottonwool, placed carefully in position and firmly sewn; then the beard and carbuncle, if any. Many of the frontal beards, moustaches and eyebrows can be made of two layers of felt stuck together and then sewn or glued flat to the face.

Now consider the expression and characterisation for the remaining features. Spend some time just looking at the figure, making a series of drawings of the expression, based on research, simplifying one drawing after another until you arrive at what you consider is the essence of the character. (Some of my early sketches accompany the patterns.) Matisse was a past master in the removal of all unnecessary detail, and you may well use him as your guide. When you are satisfied with your drawing, angle and place the eyes ('the mirror of the soul') on the head and glue them in position. Then paint in the rest of the features or apply small pieces of felt (or tightly woven cotton) for cheeks, eyelids etc. The result should aim to be the essence of, and have real respect for, the character.

Except for the characters of Pulcinella, l'Amant and Pantalone (who have their own special hats) there are two forms of hat. The first is the beret, worn by all servants in the Commedia. In most instances the rim to the beret may need gathering in a little to fit the size of the head. It should always be sewn firmly to the head, after the hair (and ears) have been sewn into position. The other basic form of hat is the flowerpot-crowned shape, with a brim of varying width. To make up the crown, cut a duplicate pattern of the sides from thin card and cover with material. Now join the sides together (using close oversewing for the entire hat). Then cover the top, making sure that the material is stretched like the top of a drum. The next stage is to make the brim. Cut a duplicate pattern from thin card and cover this on both sides with the material, oversewing both edges. Then oversew, or glue, the brim to the crown. If you use glue do not oversew the turnings on the inside perimeter of the brim but snip them all round, place to the crown, and stick the snipped turnings firmly to the inside of the crown. The hat can now be trimmed with its necessary ornamentation like hat bands, brooches, buckles and feathers. Do *not* glue or sew the hat to the head until the ears and nose have been added.

To save a lot of time, use a plastic container, such as a yoghourt-pot cut to the right size, as a foundation for the crown.

For accessories, imagination and invention are necessary so as to find a suitable convention for the making of musical instruments, swords, the clyster for le Médecin, the fan for la Bien-Aimée, and her necklace. This is where the maker must use initiative with whatever materials are available. In this collection, the musical instruments were made up basically from card and a half-circular dowel rod, then covered in fabric. The swords were based on a chopstick with gold metal-coloured card to make the hilt, adding gold braid around the edge to give it thickness. (The hilt for l'Amant's sword was adapted from a large piece of costume jewellery.) The pommels, stuck with epoxy glue to the top of the swords, were fine silver or gold pierced-metal spherical Indian beads. Brighella's dagger was fashioned from an old paper-knife with the guard adapted from part of a metal hinged belt and again stuck with the epoxy glue. La Bien-Aimée's necklace was fashioned from parts of a very large necklace with the addition of other beads and ornament. If you are lucky enough to inherit costume jewellery from your friends, the rest is yours to invent.

The entire collection of figures was designed to sit in chairs, as being the best way to display them. However, Louis XIV had to have a throne and this was fashioned from a late-eighteenth-century footstool which had seen better days. Like the figures, the chair is typical of design in France during the second half of the seventeenth century, with details simplified in keeping with the general style of the collection. The cushions, a little smaller than the seat area, were each made up in a colour and choice of fabric complementing the character, and were braided around their edges to add richness to the final result.

There is, however, no need to follow this 'seated' pattern, and the sculptures can be adapted in all sorts of ways. With a little imagination, by supporting the entire body and legs with dowel rods or heavy wire, the figures can be made to stand on a base. Marionettes and glove puppets can be modelled on the figures. Finally the description and patterns for each figure can be used as a basis for cutting and making fancy dress, or for stage costume in any play production of the period.

The patterns show some of my very first drawings after I had completed my research both from books giving their history, and the innumerable drawings or paintings of the various Commedia characters. I wanted them to look French; I did not want them to be just 'pretty' dolls. I did not want them to appear machine-made and I did not want to 'soften' the strong characterisation so typical in all the drawings of the Commedia, which has a magic world all of its own. In several instances, I took certain liberties so as to play one character strongly off against another, and there is so little information about so many of the characters that I have been forced to use conjecture and imagination. Above all else, I wanted to achieve the essence and spirit of each character as I saw it, not just a photographic copy, bearing in mind *always* the limitations of the media I was working in. To sum up, for anyone choosing to enjoy the delights of making such a collection: let your result be a personal gesture towards *your* understanding of the personality of each character. I have repeated several times the words 'characterisation', 'respect for the media', and 'individual personality'. I believe that this is the key to all crafts, letting the material determine what it wants to do, and allowing the subject to direct you to the materials needed to give it life and energy. Don't stand in the way, don't force; let it come to you, not you to it. As has been said about painting, 'When I start painting I have to remove from myself all preconceived ideas of what painting is about. There is only myself, the media, and the subject which will guide me into giving it complete and total expression'. Apply this dictum to your craft.

THE FIGVRES

MOLIÈRE
Freely based on an anonymous painting, *c.* 1670

8

MOLIÈRE

'Molière' (the pen-name of Jean-Baptiste Poquelin) was born in 1622, and died, following a long illness, a few hours after playing the role of Argan the hypochondriac in the fourth performance of his play *le Malade imaginaire*, in the year 1673. Universally accepted as the greatest writer of comedies of all time, the uniqueness of his skill and perception of human foibles and behaviour can never be overestimated.

Essentially a man of the theatre, Molière ran his own company, wrote all of their plays, and was also one of their leading actors. Poquelin first studied law, but his love of the theatre made him join a semi-professional group as an actor. The troupe found little work in Paris and took to the provinces, touring for over ten years. On these tours 'Molière' began writing comedies and may well have seen the Italian players at work, learning much from their technique and style of performance. In 1658 the company returned to Paris, with Molière as their leader, presenting his comedies at the court of Louis XIV. This time they were a success. Louis became Molière's patron; the company were given the title 'Troupe de Monsieur' after the King's brother; and they played in the Théâtre Petit-Bourbon. Years of triumph followed, and they moved to the Palais-Royal. In both theatres they played on alternate nights with the company of Italian players who, also under royal patronage, were permitted to call themselves 'Comédiens du Roi de la troupe Italienne'. Seven years after Molière died, the King formed the 'Théâtre Français', selecting many players from the survivors of Molière's company. This national company played continuously in seasons up to the French Revolution, and exists today – the oldest 'National Theatre' in Europe – as the 'Comédie-Française' still playing at the Palais-Royal.

Molière has his place in this collection as not only did he draw constantly on his observation of the Italian Troupe, but, working side by side with them and having close personal friends amongst them, he must have had an effect on their development towards scripted plays. In a sense, by reading his plays we can more readily imagine what the characters of the Commedia were like. It was said that his own acting technique was modelled on the great 'Scaramouche', Fiorilli, and, particularly in the early plays, characters very like Scaramouche, the Young Lovers, Pantalone and the Doctor regularly appear. They are still traceable in the four great comedies *l'Avare*, *Tartuffe*, *le Bourgeois gentilhomme* and *le Malade imaginaire*. In the last two of these, Molière also copied the Commedia in introducing (at a very sophisticated level) songs, dances and *entr'actes*. With Lully the resident court composer (of Italian origin) and Beauchamp the master of the dance, both the court and public theatre of Paris in the 1670s saw and heard the Commedia brought to new heights even whilst the Italian Troupe continued the improvising tradition with their own musicians and dancers.

Costume

The figure is dressed in French court costume, *c.* 1670. He wears a deep-skirted coat with tightish sleeves and breeches. Both are in the same colour. Most of the seams are covered with braid, set at regular intervals with buttons. The coat is belted and he could carry a sword and gloves. The falling collar, like his upstanding cuffs, is edged with fine lace. His stockings are of silk and the shoes have decorations placed over the insteps. He wears the typical knee-length collared cape, and the broad-brimmed high-crowned hat is decorated in front with a cockade of feathers. The hair is cut to shoulder length with a short fringe across the forehead.

Materials

Any dark and richly coloured materials can be chosen to make the costume for this figure. The final result should, above all, look elegant and stylish.

Cotton: natural colour (head, nose, hands)
        white (collar, cuffs)
Silk: deep purple (body, legs, arms, skirts, epaulettes)
     lighter purple (cape and skirt linings)
     gun-metal (stockings, body, legs, arms, skirts, epaulettes)
     bronze (cape)
     brown (shoes and their tongues)
     black watered silk (hat)
     black (knee rosettes)
Felt: brown (eyebrows, moustaches, beard, base for hair)
     white (eyes)
     pink (mouth)
Ribbon: black (kneebands) 12mm
     brocaded (belt) 15mm
     white (neckline, wrists) 12mm
     narrow black velvet (body) 6mm
Cord: black silk (skirts, epaulettes)
     grey silk (hat)
Braid: brown Russian (shoes)
Narrow lace: white (collar, cuffs) 10mm
Small black buttons: (arms, legs)
Fancy buttons: (body)
Six handsome brooches or ornaments: (shoes, kneebands, belt, hat)
Cockade of feathers: black (hat)
Jute: dull brown (hair)
Dye: black (face features)
Card: (hat)
Padding

Making

Basic Figure: Sew a 25mm band of the gun-metal-coloured silk down the centre front of the body, covering either edge with a narrow band of the black velvet ribbon. Now assemble and sew all front and all back sections together; sew the completed front body to the completed back body; turn right side out and pad. Do the same with the arms but do *not* attach them to the body.

With a 15mm band of gun-metal-coloured silk cut on the cross, cover the side seams of the body as far as the top of the stockings and the seams of the arms to the wrists. All these bands should then be decorated with the small black buttons, set evenly some 20mm apart. The fancy buttons are used on the band running down the front of the body.

Next cover the join of upper legs to stockings with a band of the black ribbon, finishing off on the outside of each leg with a small black silk rosette centred by a handsome button.

Edge the top of the shoes with the brown Russian braid, adding the tongues, with the lower edges gathered a little, and fine ornaments to the fronts.

Skirts: Line these with the lighter purple silk and edge them all round, except for the waistline, with a 12mm band of the gun-metal-coloured silk, followed by an edging of black silk cord. Place the waistline edge of the skirts to the waistline of the figure and sew in place.

Belt: The waistline is finished off with a belt of 15mm brocaded ribbon, complete with buckle, or a rich ornament, positioned at the centre front.

Arms and Epaulettes: Edge the top of the cuffs with narrow white lace, sew in the darts, join up the side, and sew the cuffs to the line where the arms meet the hands. (The cuffs will need gathering to the size of the wrists.) Cover these joins with a band of white cotton ribbon. Now sew the arms firmly to the edge of the shoulders.

Cover the shoulders with epaulettes of the deep purple silk (lined with the same material), banded all round, exactly the same as the skirts, with the gun-metal-coloured silk and the black silk cord.

Collar: Make up the collar in fine white cotton, lining it with the same material. Edge all round, save for the neckline, with the same white lace as the cuffs. Fold to the front (see pattern) the two front edges of the collar and, easing the neckline to fit the neck of the figure, sew in position. Cover this join with the white cotton ribbon, adding a bow of the same material to the centre front.

Hat: Make up the hat as described on page 6, edging the base of the crown with a thick grey silk cord. Complete by adding a cockade of black feathers and a brooch positioned at the centre front of the crown. Do not sew or glue the hat to the head until the hair and nose have been completed.

Head: Make up the three sections for the hair. Begin by looping the jute closely to the narrow bands of felt, and firmly glue it on; then cut the lower edges of the loops and unravel the jute. Next, stick the fringe to the forehead, high up. Two layers of hair are needed from the sides of the head to the back. The second layer should be stuck over the first, 10mm higher, making sure that the hat when added will cover the top felt edges of the layers of jute. Finally, trim the fringe and lengths of hair.

Make up the nose, pad it with cotton wool, and sew in position.

The hat should now be fixed firmly to the head.

Position the eyes of white felt and glue them to the face; do the same with the mouth, eyebrows, moustaches and beard. All the features – the eyes, the smile on the mouth – are painted in black.

Cape: Line the bronze silk cape with the lighter purple silk; do the same with the collar, oversewing it in position centred to the straight edge of the cape. Place on the figure, lightly catching it to the epaulettes on either side of the shoulders to keep in position.

Accessories: A folded piece of paper in his hand suggests that he may be taking notes?

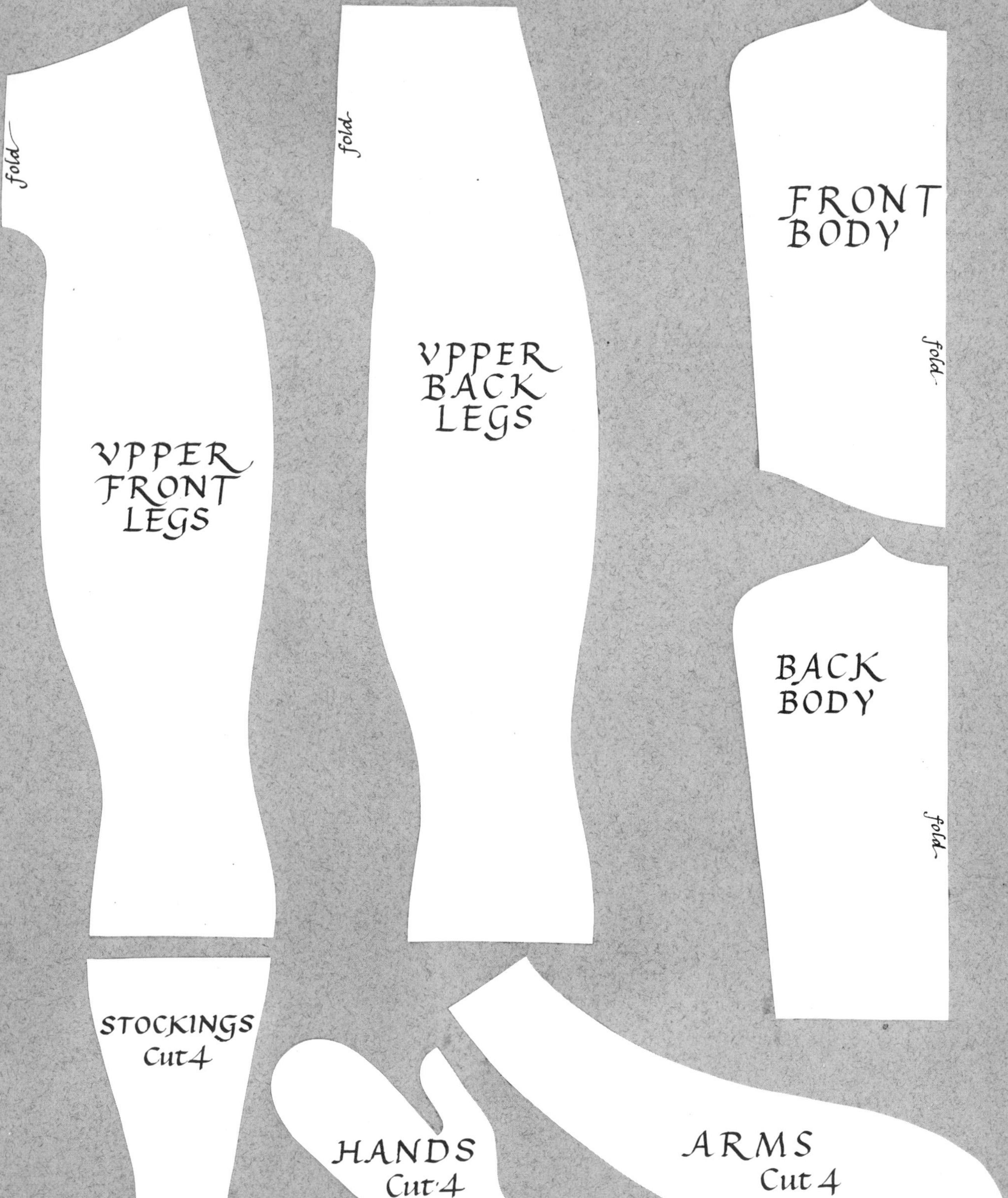

fold

UPPER
FRONT
LEGS

fold

UPPER
BACK
LEGS

FRONT
BODY

fold

BACK
BODY

fold

STOCKINGS
Cut 4

HANDS
Cut 4

ARMS
Cut 4

SHOES Cut 4

CVFFS Cut 2

dart

FRONT SKIRTS Cut 2

side seam

FRONT to COLLAR Cut 2

fold | fold

BACK to COLLAR

side seam

BACK SKIRTS

fold

EPAVLETTES Cut 2

SHOE TONGVES fold Cut 2

felt

Jute **FRINGE**

felt

HAIR TOP LAYER

Jute

felt

HAIR VNDERLAYER

Jute

BLACK

Black Wallow SILK.

Think about Tale. Get a looking ill-expression

Span Spray Arden

Antique Buttons

& Lace bow. Many Ubison painted RRR

under buttons 'HOBBY HORSE'.

PURPLE.

Bronze Size Lining

Purple black silk

woolen heel.

FACIAL EXPRESSION

GREY WAVE

silver ornament

MOLIERE.

FRONT
HEAD

fold

TOP
BACK
HEAD

fold

LOWER
BACK
HEAD

fold

SIDES of CROWN to HAT

BRIM to HAT Cut 2

GENTLE
EYES TIRED
BUT OBSERVING
SENSITIVE. VERY SIMPLE

PINK   DYE HAIR   BROWN, GREEN,
GREY.

fold centre back

TOP of
HAT

CAPE
$\frac{1}{4}$ scale

NOSE

fold

CAPE COLLAR $\frac{1}{4}$ scale

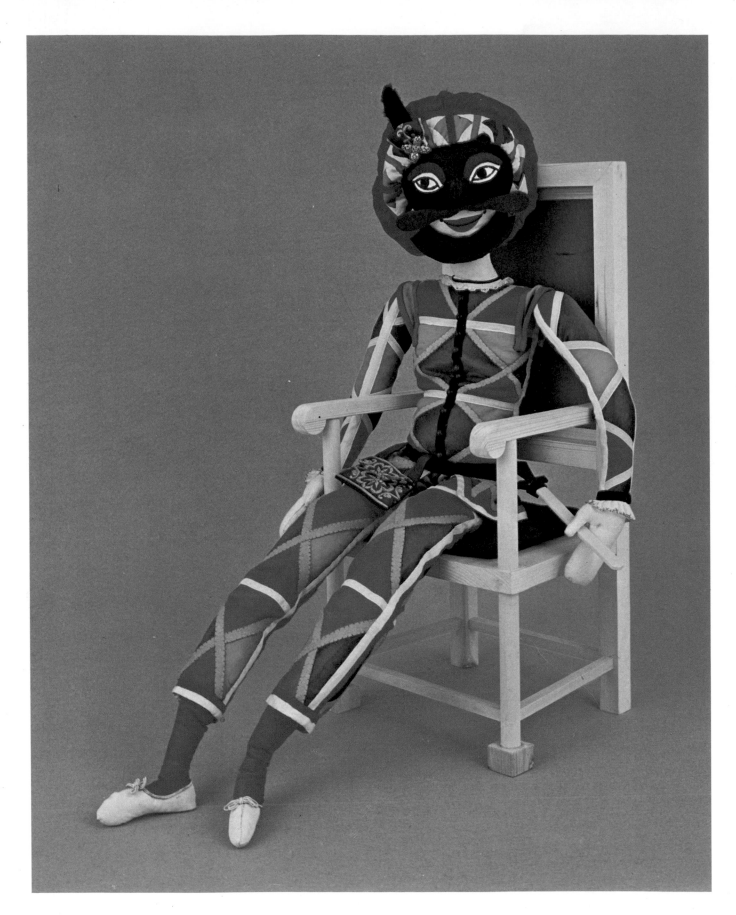

ARLEQUIN
Based on engravings and paintings *c.* 1660 to 1700

14

ARLEQUIN

Origins and Development

Well established by the second half of the sixteenth century, Harlequin may go back to the ancient art of masking, when mischievous and infernal beings were represented with blackened faces. The old Roman comedies usually included a black slave in rags, who was also the mischievous character; and it is equally possible that he is the mischievous servant 'Vice' who accompanies the devil in early Church plays. In the Commedia his native home is Bergamo in northern Italy (Arlecchino). In France, called Arlequin, one of the greatest interpreters of the role – and a great favourite of Louis XIV – was Doménique Biancolelli (1640-1688) of the Italian players in Paris. Together with Pierrot, Harlequin is still remembered in ballet, whilst Harlequinades in Christmas pantomimes and seaside summer shows were common in England until well after the end of the first World War, along with other relics of the Commedia in 'Punch and Judy' booths.

Role

The second *zanni* or servant/valet (see page 2), whose main function was to control the structure of the plot as set out in the scenarios and to hold the story line together. Within the story he might have a love affair with one of the female servants or manipulate conflicts between various other characters, but breaking into the story he commented on events, entertaining the audience with gossip, scandal and rumour about court life and some private lives. In the Italian company in Paris, he parodied the tragedies performed by the Comédie-Francaise, chatting directly to the audience like the 'stand-up' comedian of today.

Character

All things to all men, he was a rascal, a pickpocket, mercurial and quick; but able to seem lazy, clumsy and awkward or, at other times, elegant and ingenuous. Harlequin is neither young nor old but worldly wise. Some portraits show him corpulent or with a well-fed little belly overhanging his belt. Shakespeare's Autolycus and Beaumarchais' Figaro have much in common with him.

The Mask

Formerly black, bizarre and devil-like, it becomes more humanised. By 1675 it could be either a full mask with holes for the eyes and mouth, or a two-piece, the upper part covering forehead, nose and cheeks, and the lower the lower jaw. Many performers discarded the lower half. Eyebrows, moustache and beard are normally bushy, though the beard could sometimes be pointed and sometimes he even appears beardless. His nose is short. Forehead and below the eyes are frequently wrinkled. A carbuncle or protuberance sticks out from his forehead. The mask makes him look savage but as alluring as a cat.

Costume

Belted coat and trousers, originally scattered with irregular patches, become formalised into a short coat and trousers covered with geometric design of appliquéd lozenges and/or triangles in red, blue and green, all braided in either yellow or gold. The hat could be either the typical popular beret fashionable in the sixteenth century or a soft felt hat with a narrow turned-up brim in front. Often decorated with the lozenge or diamond shapes, the hat was also traditionally adorned with a feather, rabbit's scut or fox's brush which some authorities have taken to be a symbol of ridicule. The hair under the hat was always concealed by a black skullcap. A purse hangs from his belt, into which he sticks a broad wooden sword for stage 'business' – usually for whacking his adversaries on the backside. Shoes are soft, often without heels so that he can move freely into his acrobatic acts. In the Harlequinades of the nineteenth century, his costume had become simply a skin (tights and leotard) covered with the diamond pattern, a black skullcap, a black 'domino' mask which is characterless, a black 'domino' cape (shades of the devil again) – and the little wooden sword.

Movement

A mixture of mime, dance, acrobatics and tumbling. A high-jumper who could take to the air with the greatest of ease, he had to perform more acrobatics than any other character, including slackwire walking, walking on stilts or on his hands, doing back somersaults and many another gymnastic feat.

Speech, Voice and Other Skills

At first very coarse, his language and gestures were tempered by court appearances. Originally, of course, Italian-speaking, but the Harlequin Biancolelli received the King's assent to using in his act a mixture of Italian, French and a few phrases of learned Latin. Many Harlequins sang well, but in some scenarios he is to speak in an unmodulated voice like a parrot. A good mimic, his many disguises included women, gods and goddesses, doctor, beggar, lawyer – even the moon. Besides singing, he often, at different times, played the guitar, mandolin and flute. For good measure he might turn himself into a hunchback without using any padding; ride a donkey; eat, apparently, at enormous speed; and he could wield his sword with the dexterity of a military mace-bearer or the 'drum-majorette' of America and East Asia today.

Materials

Cotton: natural colour (hands and head; lower part)
Felt: black (upper head, mask)
     brown (moustaches, eyebrows, beard)
     red (mouth, hat stiffening)
Silk: red (legs, lozenges)
     green (lozenges, epaulettes)
     blue (body, arms, skirts, trousers, beret)
     soft red silk (beret, epaulette edgings)
Satin: heavy cream (shoes)
     black (belt, sword hanger)
Braid: black Russian (neckline, mask)
     cream Russian (shoes)
Brocade: blue and yellow (purse, hat cockade and rosette)
Ribbon: gold or yellow (lozenges, seams)8mm and 12mm
     narrow black velvet (body, wrists) 6mm
     narrow red (beret) 6mm

Tightly woven cotton: white (eyes)
White lace: (neck frill and wrists)
Piece of fur: (hat)
Small black buttons: (body)
Felt-covered button: (carbuncle)
Handsome button or brooch: (hat)
Buckle: (belt)
Dye: black (face)
Card: (hat)
Padding

Making

Basic Figure: Appliqé the lozenges of red and green silk to the blue silk of the front and back body shapes and arms, covering all the divisions with yellow or gold ribbon. Add a band of the black velvet ribbon with the small black buttons set at regular intervals down the centre front of the body. Assemble and sew all front and all back sections together, gathering the front body waistline towards the centre front of the leg waistline to give the slight belly when padding. Sew completed front body to completed back body, turn right side out and pad; do the same with the arms but do *not* attach them yet to the body.

Cover both the side seams of body and around the seams of the arms to the wrists with 12mm gold or yellow ribbon. Edge the top of the shoes with the cream Russian braid, adding small bows of the same braid to the fronts.

Now sew the arms firmly to the edge of the shoulders. Cover the shoulders with epaulettes of green silk (lined with the same material) banded round with red silk 6mm deep when finished. The basic figure is now complete.

Trousers: Make up according to pattern, braiding the divisions of the lozenges, and cover the side and inner leg seams in the 12mm ribbon. Gather and sew the waistline of the trousers to the waistline of the figure. Make sure that the side seams of the trousers correspond with the side seams of the body.

Skirts: After appliquéd shapes and braiding have been completed, line the skirts throughout in any of the basic colours of silk. Attach the top of the skirts to the waistline, allowing a 12mm gap at the centre front.

Belt: The waistline is finished off with a belt of black satin 20mm wide, complete with buckle. (Cut the belt 12mm shorter than the waist measurement so that when it is sewn in position it will help to accentuate the belly.)

Neckline and Wrists: Trim with a frill of white lace, terminating at the neck with a band of black Russian braid and at the wrists with the black velvet ribbon.

Hat: Make up the hatband with the lozenges braided, stiffening the back with red felt. Gather the top part of the beret – in soft red silk – evenly to the top edge of the band, covering the seam with narrow red ribbon. Mount the piece of fur to represent the fox's brush on thin card (or felt) to keep it upright, and sew on. Decorate the base with a cockade and rosette made from the blue and yellow brocade, and finish off with a handsome button or brooch.

Now leave the hat until the head is complete, save for the eyes, mouth, and other features.

Head and Mask: Sew up the centre front seam, then ease the mask, gathering it to the side seams of the face and terminating line below the cheeks as in the pattern. Pad firmly (but imaginatively), stretching the felt to the expression you want. Finish off the lower edge of the mask with black Russian braid. Sew together the two black felt crescents to make the lower part of the mask and firmly pad it; glue and/or sew this section to the chin line of the head.

Cut moustaches and beard from two thicknesses of brown felt, glued together to stiffen and control their shapes; glue them in position immediately under the nose and under the curve of the lower edge of the mask respectively. Should the final result be limp, add another layer of felt.

Now return to the hat. Softly pad the beret to control its shape and to add extra bulk to the back of the head, and glue or sew in position. Depending on the finished shape of the head, the edge of the beret may need to be eased to fit.

Glue mouth in position, painting the smile in with black dye (or poster colour if dye is difficult). Add features to the eyes with black dye or paint; be careful to place the eyes on the head to see that they have the right wicked expression before glueing them. Then glue the brown felt eyebrows in place and, making the carbuncle from a largish button surrounded by cottonwool and covered with brown felt, sew it high in position on the forehead to complete the figure.

Accessories: Make the sword hanger from two strips of black satin, lined with the same; hang it from the waistline and sew it to the horizontal strip which (when joined A to A) forms the slot to carry the sword. Any thin wood can be cut to make the sword. Finally, the purse made from blue and yellow brocade, lined with the same, is formed by joining the side seams (A to B) allowing the flap to fold forwards. Sew the top edges of the two vertical strips to the top edge of the belt and the sculpture is complete.

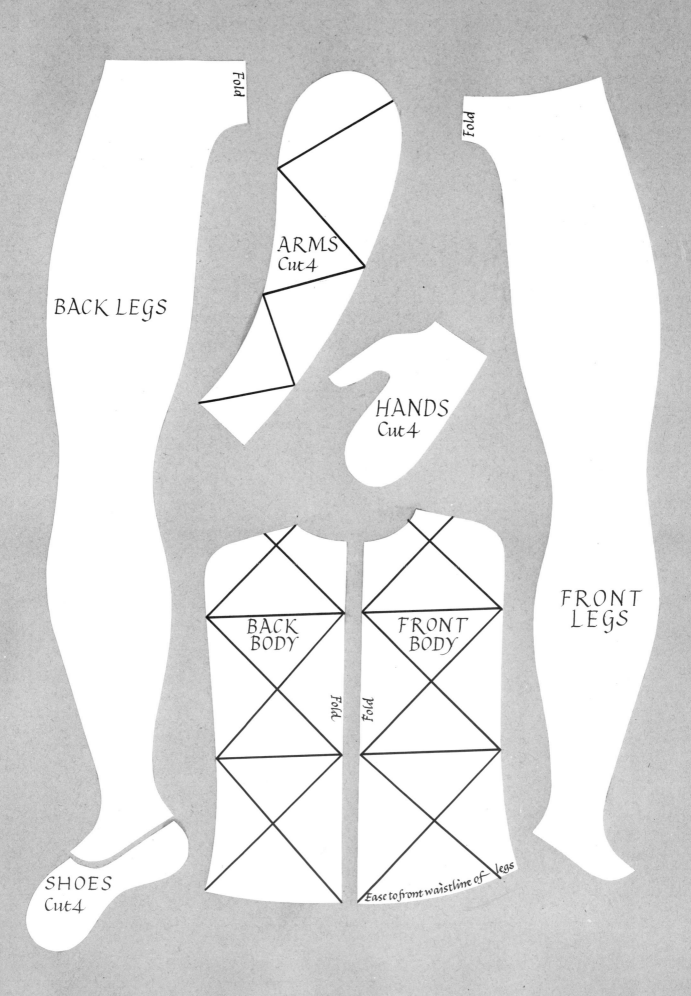

BACK LEGS

Fold

ARMS
Cut 4

HANDS
Cut 4

Fold

FRONT
LEGS

BACK
BODY

Fold

Fold

FRONT
BODY

SHOES
Cut 4

Ease to front waistline of legs

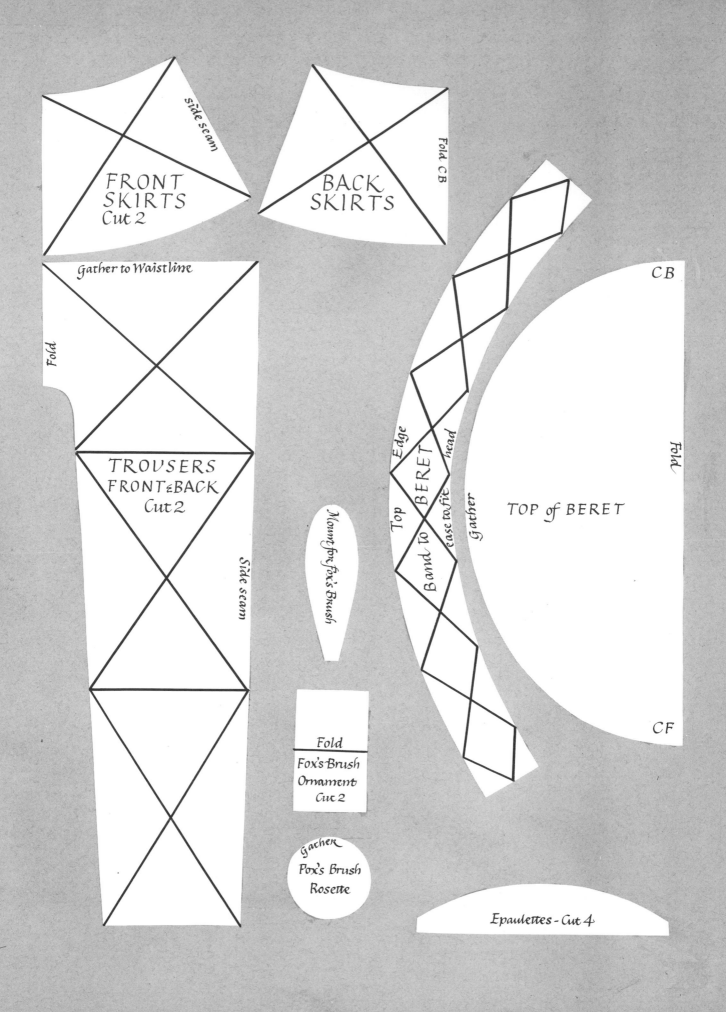

FRONT
SKIRTS
Cut 2

Side seam

BACK
SKIRTS

Fold CB

Gather to Waistline

Fold

TROUSERS
FRONT & BACK
Cut 2

Side seam

Mount for Fox's Brush

Fold

Fox's Brush
Ornament
Cut 2

Gather

Fox's Brush
Rosette

Top Edge

BERET

Band to ease to fit head

Gather

CB

Fold

TOP of BERET

CF

Epaulettes - Cut 4

MASK
Cut 2

ease and gather to sides and front of head

CF

FRONT HEAD
Cut 2

Positioning of top part of mask

positioning of lower part of mask

CF

BACK of HEAD
Cut 2

CB   X

SIDE BACK of HEAD
Cut 2

side seam

X

EYES - Cut 2

MOUSTACHES - Cut 2

Lower section of mask cut 2

BEARD - cut 2

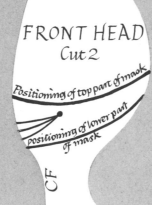

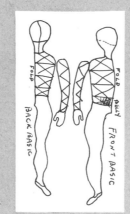

FOLD   BACK BASIC

FOLD BELLY   FRONT BASIC

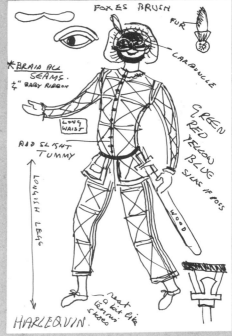

FOXES BRUSH

FUR

BRAID ALL SEAMS.
¼" BABY RIBBON

CARBUNCLE

LONG WAIST

ADD SLIGHT TUMMY

LONGISH LEGS

GREEN
RED
YELLOW
BLUE
SILKS IF POSS

WOOD

neat a bit like *tennis* shoes

HARLEQUIN.

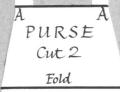

A   A

PURSE
Cut 2

Fold

B   B

Fold Forward

Sword Hanger Cut 2

Sword Hanger Cut 2

A   Sword Hanger Cut 2   A

START WITH BASIC HEAD AND ADD OUT

KEEP ARM JOIN ONLY AT TOP FOR FLEXIBILITY.

(FIND ORNAMENT FOR FINISHING OFF FOX BRUSH

SWORD

BRIGHELLA

Based on a print by Bonnart (*c.* 1675)

BRIGHELLA

Origins and Development

Briga (= trouble maker) may be traced back to the old Atellan farces, playing the 'villain' of the piece. He originates from the town of Bergamo in Northern Italy: some even claim that he came from the upper city where the inhabitants were supposed to be craftier, coarser and more cunning. By 1670 he was at the height of his popularity in Paris.

Role

The first *zanni*, and originally the most important servant role in the comedy, he guides the action, creating tension and conflict by his constant intrigues and the suspicions of his motives formed by the other characters. He believes in no half measures: 'When you lie or deceive let it be worthwile'. As the senior manipulator and motivator in enriching the plot, he uses all his calculated cunning to outwit as many as he possibly can.

Character

Sharp-witted, unscrupulous and cynical; robs, fights and steals; flatters and lies with malice. Murder is nothing to Brighella, but even with his bloodthirstiness he has the ability to charm. He will serve any person who will pay him – soldiers, wealthy merchants etc. He is also a perjurer and debaucher, who will always play the innocent with anyone who tries to unmask his villainy.

The Mask

He wears the full or half mask – sometimes with a separate chin-piece like Arlequin, the expression animal-like and usually in olive green: sly slit eyes, sensual lips and a bulbous or beak-like nose. A dandy when it comes to his raven locks, beard and moustaches, his fine and curly black hair is oiled and pomaded; the moustaches are waxed to a sharp point and so is his beard which covers most of his lower jaw.

Costume

Originally a loose white tunic and trousers and a floppy white hat, but by the beginning of the seventeenth century it had become more or less standardised – a uniform or livery all of white and banded or braided with stripes of green (white has always been associated with purity, and green with evil, shrouded in mystery). The white-skirted tunic, belted, is buttoned down the fronts which are banded with strips of green that also stripe the sides of the sleeves. A small white collar decorates the throat. The trousers are loose and on the short side – these too are banded on the side seams with green. The knee-length cape with semi-circular collar is of white or possibly green; bands of white and green decorate the sides of the cloak like the rest of his costume. The hat is a white beret ornamented with bands of green. In his belt he carries his purse and a sharply-pointed, dangerous dagger. He is often pictured carrying a gaily-ribboned guitar.

Movement

A swaggerer – he moves his arms and legs in a rhythmical way. He also prowls with gliding movements like a cat, with eyes always at work – sharp and piercing, penetrating like those of the alley cat, quiet and ready to pounce, then vanish.

Speech, Voice and Other Skills

The language, very vulgar and coarse, is a bastard dialect of Bergamo. Speech is soft and low but he can imitate with his voice an entire orchestra. He sings and dances well, and amongst instruments other than the guitar he plays the theorbo, lute and psaltery. In the scenarios he often appears in disguise, like so many of the other characters in the Commedia.

Materials

Cotton: natural colour (neck and body, arms)
    white (tunic, skirts, sleeves, trousers, cape, beret)
    green glazed (cape and collar, epaulettes, lining to skirts)
    soft white (Peter Pan collar)
    heavy green (shoes)
    patterned (guitar)
Corduroy: brown (belt)
    patterned (purse)
Jersey: striped (mask and nose)
Silk: brown (epaulettes)
Satin: yellow (guitar)
Brocade: green (beret)
Lurex: striped black and gold (guitar)
Felt: dark green (guitar)
    black (face features, guitar)
    white (eyes, mouth)
Bias binding: green (tunic, sleeves, skirts, beret, trousers, cape) 12mm
Braid: green Russian (shoes)
Ribbon: blue velvet (collar) 6mm
    dark brown (tunic) 12mm
    black (shoes) 12mm
    green and blue streamers (guitar) 12mm
Lace: white (epaulettes, sleeves, collar) 10mm
Suede: blue (neckline)
Silk upholstery fringe: black (hair)
Small black buttons: (body)
Two black cloth-covered buttons: (shoes)
Dye: black, green and yellow (face features)
Card: (guitar)
Semi-circular dowel rod: (guitar)
Dagger
Padding

Making

First take all the nine sections of white cotton which are braided in green and apply to all these surfaces the green bias binding (as indicated on the patterns). Then sew each of these sections to the appropriate parts of the tunic, skirts, sleeves, trousers, and beret (which are all cut from the same basic white cotton). The cape banding is sewn to the cape of green glazed cotton. *The seaming and folding is indicated on all the patterns.*

Basic Figure: Assemble and sew all front and all back sections together, gathering the front body waistline to the front of the leg waistline to provide the belly when padding. Sew completed front body to completed back body, turn right side out and pad.

Do the same with the arms; then make up the sleeves, which should terminate with narrow bands of white lace around the lower edges. Place sleeves on the arms and gather the heads to the top of the arms, simulating the shape of an armhole. When finished, the outer fold line of the sleeves should balance with the outer seams of the arms. Do *not* attach the completed arms to the body.

Edge the top of the shoes with the green Russian braid, adding black ribbon bows to the fronts, centred with a small black cloth-covered button.

Trousers: Make up the trousers, hemming the ends of the legs; place on the figure, gathering the waistline to fit the body. Making sure that the side folds of the trousers correspond with the side seams of the outside of the legs, sew in position.

Tunic: Add a narrow band of dark brown ribbon with small black buttons set at regular intervals down the centre front of the body. Now sew the front and back together, leaving the shoulder-line sufficiently open at the neck edge for placing the tunic on to the body. When this has been done, finish sewing up the shoulder seams and sew the neckline to the figure. Lastly, sew the waistline edge to the figure, gathering the front so that the side seams match the side seams of the body.

Skirts: Line the skirts with the green glazed cotton; gather the top of the skirts to the waistline, leaving a 6mm gap at the centre front, and sew in position.

Belt and Purse: Sew up the side seams of the patterned corduroy purse and gather fairly tightly, as indicated on pattern; sew to the right hand side of the body waistline, making sure that the top edge of the purse will be seen when the belt has been positioned.

Make up the belt in brown corduroy, 15mm deep, and sew it to the body at the join of tunic to skirts.

Arms and Epaulettes: Now firmly sew the finished arms to the body, commencing at the edge of the shoulders. Cover the shoulders with epaulettes of green glazed cotton (lined with the same material) banded round the curved edges with brown silk 6mm deep; the straight edges are finished off with a band of the narrow white lace.

Neckline: Make up the Peter Pan collar, lining it with the same material, and edge it with the narrow white lace; ease and sew to the neckline of the tunic, finishing off the neck edge with a narrow band of blue suede. A neat blue velvet ribbon bow decorates the centre front.

Hat: Make up the beret rim in green brocade, stiffening the back with felt. Now ease and sew the striped band, top edge, to the circumference of the white cotton beret. Gather the lower edge of the striped band evenly to the beret rim. Now leave the hat until the nose and the hair have been sewn to the head.

Head and Hair: Unravel the black silk upholstery fringe and sew both layers to the sides and back of the head, making sure that when the beret is placed in position it will cover the top edge of the line of the fringe. Trim the lower edge of the fringe neatly all round. Make up the nose, pad it with soft cotton wool, and sew in position.

The beret can now be sewn or glued to the head, placing it high on the forehead. It is advisable to fill the inside of the beret with softly crushed-up pieces of tissue paper to help it to retain its shape. Depending on the finished shape of the head, the edge of the beret may need to be eased to fit.

Now position carefully all the face features (eyes, eyebrows, frown, moustaches, mouth and beard) and glue to the head. The moustaches and the beard should be cut from two thicknesses of the black felt, glued together to stiffen and control their shapes; the moustaches should only be fixed to the very centre of the face immediately below the nose, and the beard only at the top where it meets the mouth.

Lastly, paint in the features – yellow eyes and black pupils, black eyelids, and black defining the teeth. To give a more animal expression, paint the lower and part of the upper eyelids in green.

Cape: Line in the same material up to the commencement of the folded band of white and green. (The band of green and white stripes, when finished, should be of the same width on both the outside and inside of the cape.)

The green glazed cotton collar, lined with the same material, is positioned centrally to the straight edge of the cape and then firmly oversewn. Place the finished cape on the figure, keeping it in position by lightly catching it on either shoulder seam of the epaulettes.

Guitar: Cut the top and bottom surfaces of the guitar out of firm card and cover with the patterned cotton, glueing the turnings on the back of the card. (The turnings will need snipping all round to make them follow the curves of the card and lie flat when glued.) Make up the sides with card covered with yellow satin, and closely oversew the top and bottom edge of the sides to the top and bottom edges of the guitar.

Glue to the top surface a circle of black felt and a narrow band of dark green felt all around the edge. The fingerboard is a length of semi-circular dowel rod covered with the striped Lurex – the stripes simulating the guitar strings – firmly glued, with an epoxy glue, to the other part of the instrument. Now sew a bunch of green and blue ribbons to the top of the fingerboard and a length of ribbon or cord to the base of the guitar, which will keep the finished instrument in position on the figure.

Lastly, angle the guitar well down on the right side of the figure, with the top of the fingerboard on the same level as the left shoulder, passing the cord around the back (under the cape). Then glue the left hand in position, with the fingerboard between the thumb and fingers.

Dagger: The final result should look pointed and menacing. The sculpture shown uses part of a small pointed paper-knife for the blade, part of a silver buckle for the guard, and a short length of brass rod, which luckily terminated in a knob, for the hilt. All these sections were stuck together with the epoxy glue, which also secures the dagger between the thumb and fingers of the right hand.

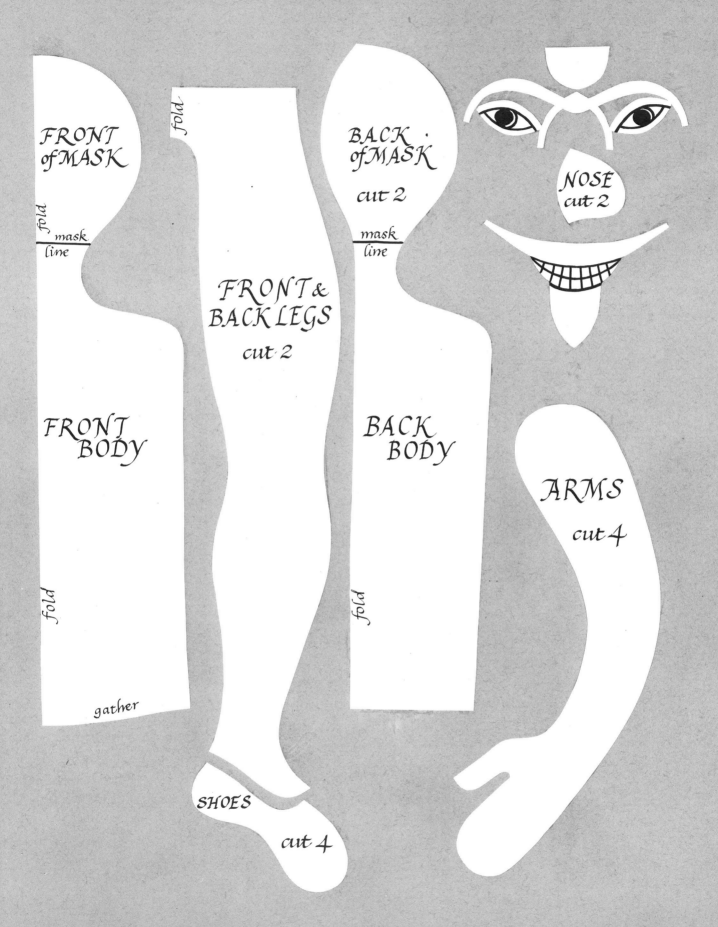

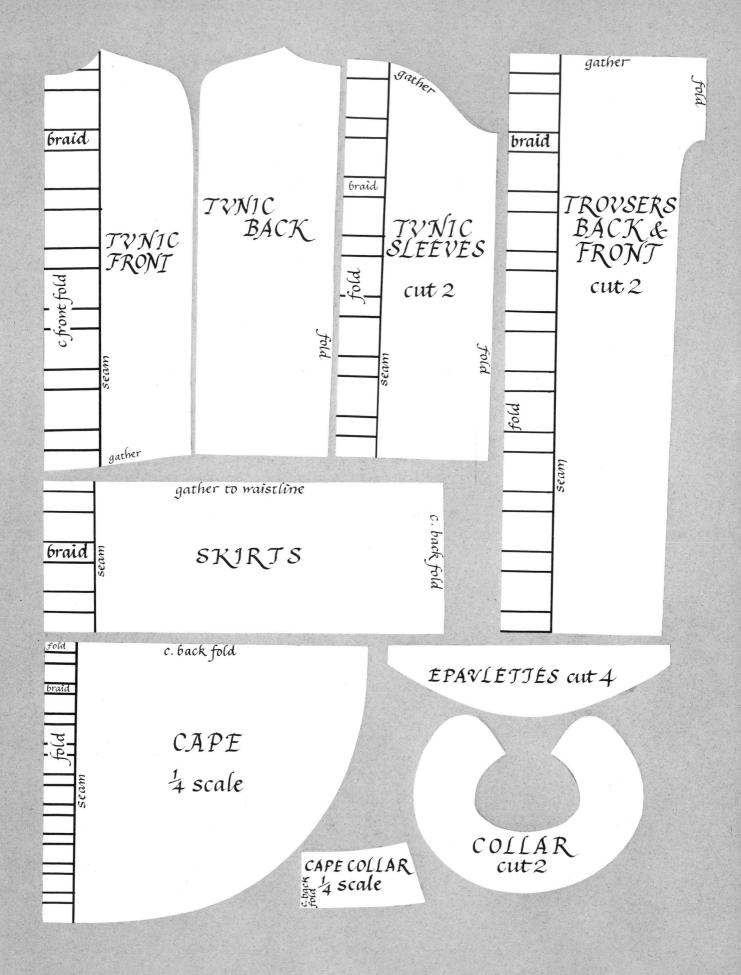

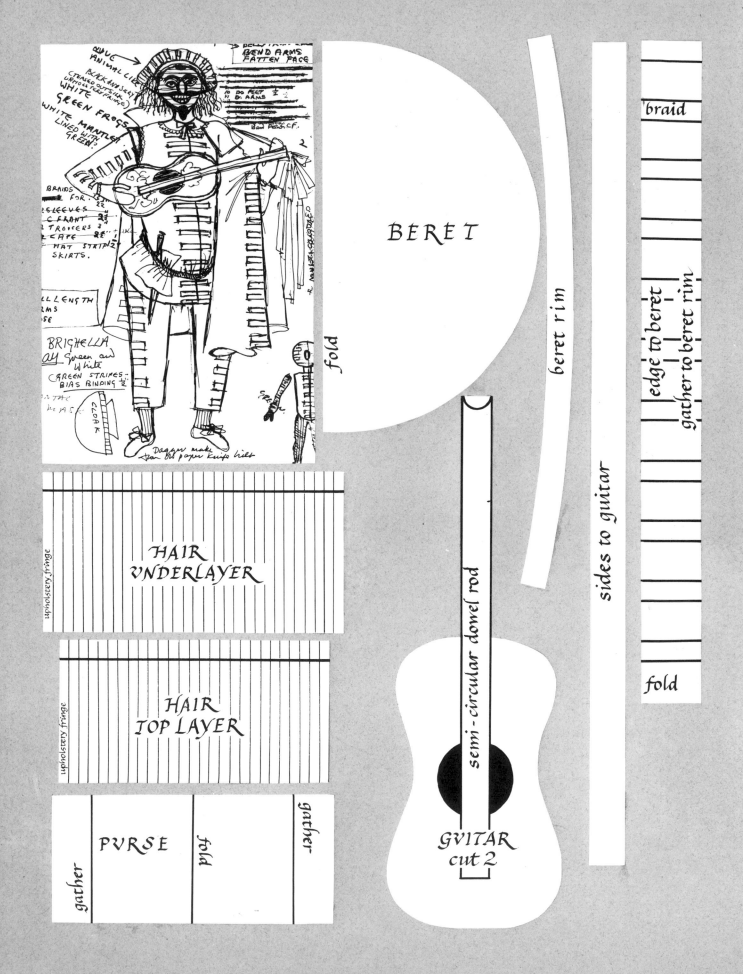

BERET

fold

braid

edge to beret

gather to beret rim

beret rim

sides to guitar

fold

HAIR
UNDERLAYER

upholstery fringe

HAIR
TOP LAYER

upholstery fringe

PURSE

gather

fold

gather

semi-circular dowel rod

GUITAR
cut 2

PANTALONE
Based on the traditional costume

PANTALONE

Origins and Development

Pantalone could claim kinship with the ancient improvised *Phylakes* (the 'gossip players'), the written comedies of Aristophanes, the Atellan farces (in which he could have played Pappus, a blockhead of a father), and the written comedies of Plautus and Terence. He undoubtedly stems from the old phallic comedies, as early illustrations of this character in the Italian comedy show him wearing a mighty erect cod-piece (phallus), and his nose and beard emphasise this symbolism.

Shakespeare writes of the 'lean and slippered Pantalone' (*As You Like It*) and, as we have seen, Molière uses the character in many plays. In England, his theatrical descendant appeared in many a Restoration comedy: Sir Anthony Absolute in *The Rivals* is a good, late example; and he is not unrecognisable in the north country settings of J.B. Priestly and television soap opera wherever the 'older generation' father is written in.

Role

A leading character, many of the scenarios centre around Pantalone as a symbol of the establishment and the older generation, representing a very wealthy (or, at times, impecunious) Venetian merchant. He is often attended by several servants and is a constant companion (or sworn enemy, for both are mean when it comes to money matters) of the Doctor, whom he frequently wishes to marry off to his daughter, much against her will. Sometimes he plays the rival to his own son; usually he is a widower, but when he has a wife she usually takes sides with the young people. At the conclusion of the comedy he more often than not relents and approves of his daughter's choice of a young man of good breeding, allowing them to marry – the old generation giving way to the new. Pantalone is the first 'old man' of the comedies. He is in his sixties.

Character

Although old, and really senile, he is amorous, lecherous and lusty below his years, trying to pass himself off as youthful in his behaviour and referring to himself as 'a randy old goat'. A lover of pomp and extravagance, he is cunning and hot tempered, often putting himself into a violent fury. He will get into an argument at a moment's notice. He loves flattery and can appear kind but gruff – his bark is frequently worse than his bite. He curses: 'When you go into the country may the snakes bite you, the wasps sting you, the bulls gore you!' etc. Dominating his household, he wants everything his own way. By the mid-eighteenth century, the character becomes a more honest and respected elderly citizen.

The Mask

The traditional colour for the mask is brown. Taking liberties with this colour, it has here been changed to red, as being the dominant colour of his characterisation in costume. The mask terminates below the cheeks. The nose is hooked and long. The eyebrows and moustaches are heavy, the beard invariably long and pointed; their colour is white streaked with grey, untidy like his long white head of hair flowing out, sometimes below shoulder length, beneath his cap.

Costume

Pantalone's dress shows a direct influence from the Near Eastern countries. His black, short-sleeved Persian or Turkish robe is lined with red, his simple, brimless Greek cap is of felt or wool; and he has turned-up-toed Turkish yellow mules or slippers (hence Shakespeare's description). He wears a red, skirted, short-waisted doublet, fastening down the front, which emphasises the length of his thin, 'lean' legs. The sleeves are tight, and both wrists and neckline are sometimes finished off with cuffs and a falling collar. He wears either tight braided breeches of red with red stockings, or tights (or tightly-fitting trousers) covering his feet (hence 'Pantaloons' – long tight-fitting trousers replacing the breeches of the eighteenth century). The figure wears a chain about his neck terminating in a rich medallion, and a belt to carry his purse. In some scenarios he also carries a sword.

Movement

Slow, often holding his hands behind his back under the robe. But he can suddenly become very agile, including backfalls and collapsing to the ground on hearing bad news. The facial expression is very mobile and constantly changes with his passions as he harangues those who oppose him, twitching his moustaches and eyebrows and wagging his beard (which he often thrusts forward, jutting out his head to accentuate his hunched-up shoulders). With his long thin legs, he takes long strides, stalking with emphasised stiff knee movements. Often the actor played the part in profile, revealing his silhouette to best advantage. (Groucho Marx did much the same thing, knowingly or not.)

Speech, Voice and Other Skills

He speaks eloquently in the Venetian dialect with a harsh nasal voice, often accompanied by a rough strident laugh. He is given to bouts of panting. Pantalone sings, sometimes in duet with his servant, accompanying himself on either the lute or the mandolin.

Materials

Wool: deep purple, red (body, skirts, arms)
Silk: brilliant rose (stockings)
     bright red (mask, ears)
     deep red (hat)
     scarlet (purse)
     rough silk-yellow (slippers)
Satin: red-purple (upper legs)
Cotton crepe: black (robe)
Cotton: white (face, beard)
     natural colour (neck, hands)
Felt: red (mouth)
     deep red (cheeks)
     white (eyebrows, moustaches, eyes, hair, fringe)
Ribbon: black (hat) 8mm
     red (upper legs) 8mm
Braid: ornamental deep red of various widths (body, belt, wrists, kneebands)
     yellow Russian (slippers)

Antique lace: cream (neck and wrist frills) 65mm and 22mm
Cotton upholstery fringe: white (hair) 75mm
Three gold studs: (kneebands, purse)
Gold tassel: (purse)
Chain and fine medallion: (neck)
Card: (hat)
Padding

Making

Basic Figure: Add a band of red braid (15mm wide) to the centre front of the body. Assemble and sew all front and all back sections together, then sew the completed front body to completed back body, turn right side out and pad. Do the same with the arms but do *not* attach them to the body.

Cover the side seams of the body with the red braid, and the side seams of the legs as far as the top of the stockings with the narrow red ribbon. Cover the join of the upper legs to the stockings with narrow red braid, finishing off with a gold stud sewn to the outside seams. Edge the top of the slippers with the yellow Russian braid.

With the narrow cream lace make up the gathered wrist frills, sewing them to the join of arms to hands; then cover this join with a band of the narrow red braid. Now sew the arms firmly to the edge of the shoulders. The basic figure is complete.

Skirts: Line the skirts in red silk. Attach the top of the skirts to the waistline, allowing a 25mm gap at the centre front. (The skirts may need easing to form this division.)

Belt: The waistline is finished off with a belt 15mm wide, made up out of red braid.

Neck Frill: Trim the neckline with a deep frill of cream antique lace, making sure that the gathering is full and not mean.

Hat and Hair: Make up the pill-box-shaped hat in deep red silk (stiffening the sides with thin card), adding a band of black narrow silk ribbon to the sides of the hat, 25mm up from the base. The hat may need to be bigger or smaller in circumference depending on the amount of padding you have placed in the head.

Now add the hair. First cut a narrow fringe from the white felt and glue it to the front of the hat; it should terminate at the side seams of the head when the hat is placed in position. The back hair, commencing from the termination of the fringe, is made up from a strip of unravelled white cotton upholstery fringe and then glued to the back of the hat. Place the finished hat well to the back of the head and glue or sew in position.

Robe: Line each section of the black crepe robe, with the exception of the collar, in the red silk. Do *not* join the hems of the lining to the hems of the robe itself; let them hang independently when finished.

Now join up the yoke to the back, the side seams and the shoulder seams with close over-sewing; then sew up the sleeves, gathering them to fit the armholes and oversew in position.

The collar, unlined, is hemmed all round, then gathered at the neck edge and oversewn to the neckline of the robe. It should finish on either side of the fronts about 30mm down from the shoulder seams. Place the finished robe on the figure and lightly catch, on either shoulder, to keep it in position.

Head and Mask: First make up each ear in two thicknesses of the red silk interlined with felt to stiffen them, paint in the features with black, and sew them to the sides of the head beginning at the commencement of the hat.

Now, angling the eyes down towards the nose, glue them in position, followed by the dark red felt cheek features. Paint in black the eyes, eyelids and the lines beneath the eyes.

Cut the moustaches and eyebrows from two thicknesses of white felt glued together to stiffen and control their shapes; glue them down *only* at the centre of the head; the eyebrows come immediately at the top of the nose and the moustaches immediately under it. The red felt mouth is then glued immediately under the moustache. The remaining features are painted in black: a strong frown above the centre of the eyebrows, the chin, and a line under the lips which should turn down on either side of the face at the corners of the mouth to give a bad-tempered expression.

Purse: Line throughout in the same material (scarlet silk) and join up side seams on either side (X to O). Fold the flap forward to the front, finishing it off with a gold tassel and a gold stud or button. Now fold *back* the two supporting bands and sew the ends to the top edge of the purse. Place to the belt on the right side of the figure and sew in position.

Accessories: The chain of office is made from a small gold chain terminating with a fine medallion or part of a handsome brooch.

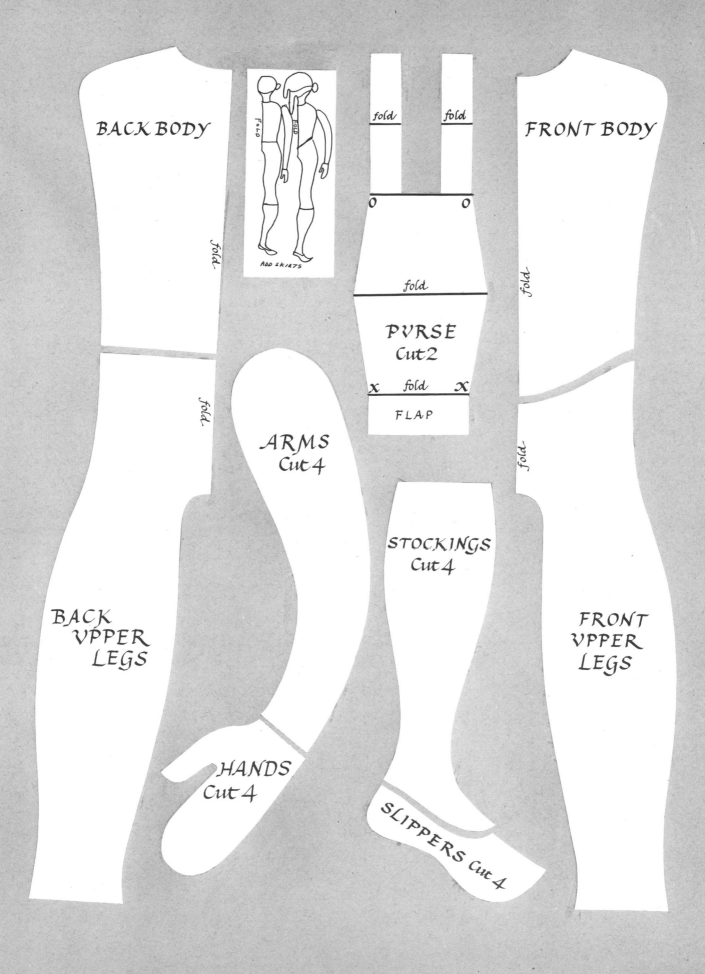

BACK BODY

FRONT BODY

fold

fold

fold

fold

fold   fold

0   0

fold

PVRSE
Cut 2

x   fold   x

FLAP

FOLD   FOLD

ADD SKIRTS

ARMS
Cut 4

STOCKINGS
Cut 4

BACK
VPPER
LEGS

FRONT
VPPER
LEGS

HANDS
Cut 4

SLIPPERS Cut 4

COLLAR to ROBE
¼ scale

gather to neckline

YOKE BACK
of ROBE ¼ scale

BACK of ROBE
¼ scale

SLEEVES to ROBE
¼ scale

gather

FRONTS
to ROBE
Cut 2

¼ scale

side seam

BACK SKIRTS

side seam

side seam

FRONT SKIRTS
Cut 2

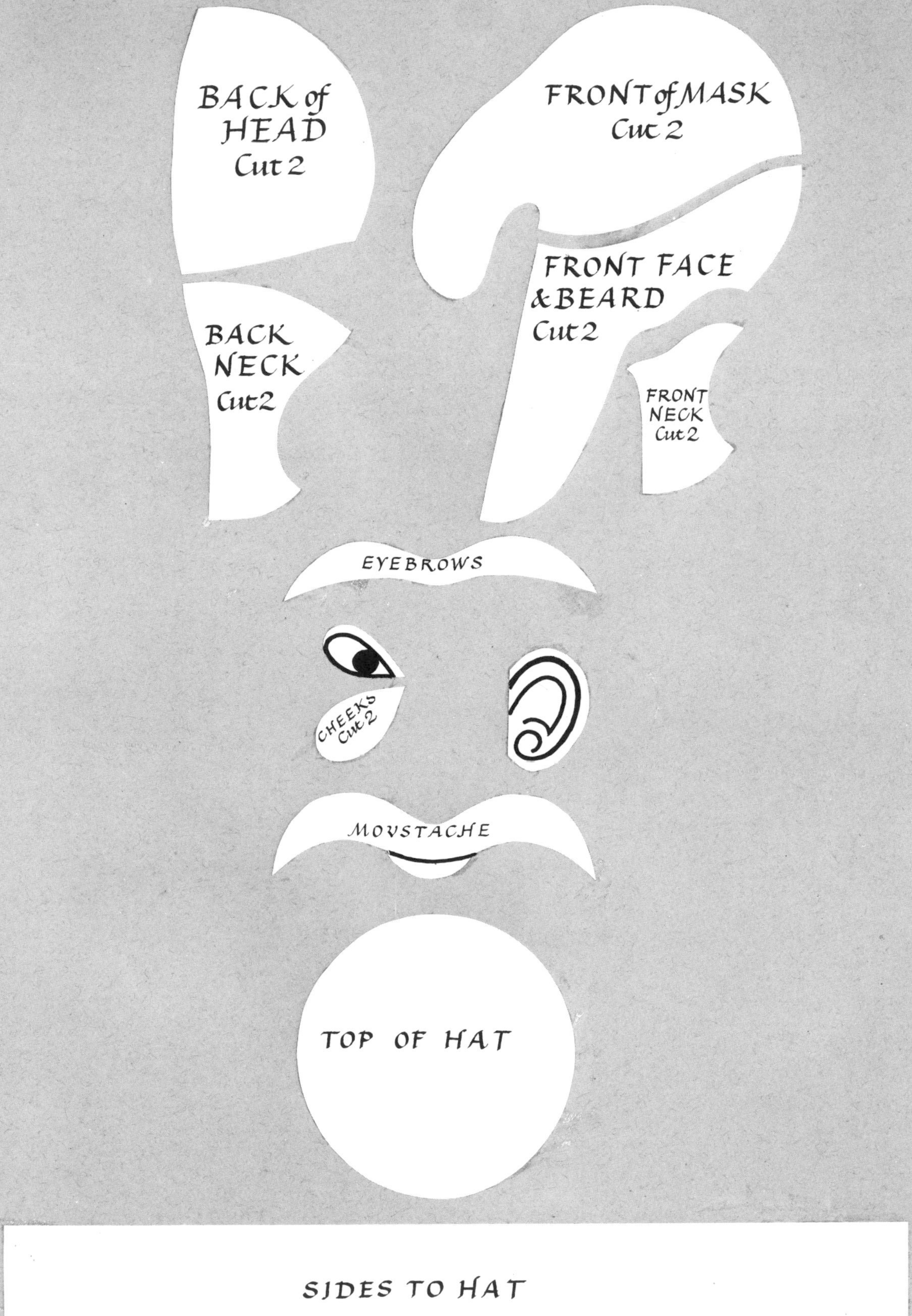

BACK of
HEAD
Cut 2

FRONT of MASK
Cut 2

BACK
NECK
Cut 2

FRONT FACE
& BEARD
Cut 2

FRONT
NECK
Cut 2

EYEBROWS

CHEEKS
Cut 2

MOVSTACHE

TOP OF HAT

SIDES TO HAT

LE MÉDECIN
Based on the traditional costume

LE MÉDECIN

Origins and Development

He comes from the university town of Bologna in northern Italy. Well established by the late sixteenth century, the characterisation, role and costume changed very little during the history of the Italian players. Molière frequently used the Doctor as an individual character in a leading role, and even caricatured a group of 'Doctors' in *le Malade imaginaire*, similar to today's chorus in a musical.

Role

The 'second old man' in the comedy, he usually accompanies Pantalone, or sometimes acts as a rival in a love encounter. Philosopher and pedant, he satirises the elderly members of the establishment (in particular the doctor and physician), but he also has a 'knowledge' of languages, astrology, grammar, law, philosophy and, of course, anatomy. These subjects he can carry on about for hours on end. A very important role in the comedies, he helps on or messes up the schemes of Pantalone with his never-ending bombastic tirades, in strong contrast to the mimetic contributions of many of the other characters. The Doctor is often a figure of ridicule, and is frequently cuckolded by the servants and the young lovers.

Character

The Doctor loves his own long speeches and the sound of his voice. Thick skinned, and incapable of ever being proved wrong, he gets his medical diagnoses and facts (which are anyway completely incomprehensible to those concerned) in a chaotic meaningless muddle. Most situations are dominated by his pomposity – but not all. Shrewd where money is concerned, he is also lecherous and always anxious for a love encounter. He is stout, slow, and has an enormous eating-capacity.

The Mask

The mask, usually flesh-coloured with a red nose, varies considerably. It could cover the upper part of the face including the cheeks; sometimes it covered only the forehead and nose; sometimes it was just a large false nose, beaky and bulbous, maybe disfigured by a red wart. Some actors discarded the mask altogether; but whether wearing the mask or not, the actor always reddened his cheeks. Many interpreters, at their discretion, did not wear the pointed beard and moustaches and appeared clean-shaven.

In this interpretation, the expression on his face is a mixture of gravity, severity and pomposity with the eyes bright and searching. He could equally be sculptured as the original 'red-nosed comedian'.

Costume

He wears the costume of the academic doctor, black with occasional touches of white. The black-skirted jacket is buttoned through and belted at the waistline. In the belt, he always carried a purse for prescriptions and fees, and a large white handkerchief to comfort or stem wounds. The neckline is finished off with a deep white collar or wide gathered frill, with the jacket sleeves ending in narrow or deep cuffs, also in white. The black breeches are full, gathered in at the knees and fastened with ties or buckles. The stockings are black like his shoes, which are simple, heeled, and buckled, or fastened with ribbon ties. The hair is hidden – as with so many of the other characters – by the black skull cap.

The black hat is wide-brimmed and often floppy but turned up in front. As an alternative he can substitute for this hat an enormous black academic beret; both are plain and sparse in any form of ornament. As part of his 'uniform' he always wears an enormous black cloak, or more traditionally the black 'magister' robe of the academic. One of his props for stage business, always good for a laugh, was his clyster (enema): he could also carry gloves.

Movement

Clumsy, heavy and pompous in his formality, he walks, however, with tiny mincing steps, his body swaying to and fro in contrast to the long stalking strides of Pantalone. He loves gesticulating with his arms and hands to emphasise a point in argument or in one of his long bursts of oratory.

Speech, Voice and Other Skills

He speaks with a lisping voice in a dialect of Bologna and in classical Italian – with a lot of 'mumbo-jumbo' passages spoken in Latin or Greek, usually wrongly pronounced and always meaningless. He loves the sound of his own voice and never likes to stop once he has got started – much to the annoyance of Pantalone, who also likes to pursue his own views and opinions relentlessly, leading to great tension and frustration between the two actors in confrontation.

Materials

Cotton: black (skullcap back, body through to stockings, arms, skirts)
  fine white (handkerchief, neck frills, cuffs)
  natural colour (neck, ears)
  grey (lining to fronts of academic robe)
Brushed cotton: black (stockings, breeches)
Cotton corduroy: brown (belt) 22mm band
Cotton velvet: black (academic robe)
Watered silk: black (hat)
Silk: black (shoes, lining of academic robe)
  grey (gloves)
Ribbed silk: red (face)
Satin: black (purse)
Felt: grey (hatband)
  brown (beard)
  dark brown (moustaches, eyebrows)
  red (mouth)
  white (eyes)
  deep blue (body and skirts) 15mm band
Ribbon: black (knee bows, shoe ties) 12mm
  indigo blue (wrists and kneebands) 12mm
Braid: black Russian (shoes)
Suede: grey-blue (purse)
Small black buttons: (body, skirts)

Covered black button: (purse)
Black dye: (face features)
Card: (hat)
Padding

Making

Basic Figure: Add a band of deep blue felt with the small black buttons set at regular intervals down the centre front of the body. Assemble and sew all front and all back sections together, then sew the completed front body to completed back body, turn right side out and pad.

Do the same with the arms, adding gathered upstanding cuffs, in white cotton, to the wrists. Cover join of cuffs to the wrists with a band of indigo blue cotton ribbon. The arms are now complete but do *not* attach them to the body.

Edge the top of the shoes with the black Russian braid, adding small black cotton ribbon bows to the fronts.

Breeches: Make up the breeches in black brushed cotton and place them on the figure, sewing and gathering the waist edge evenly to the waistline of the body, and the ends of the legs to the top of the stockings. Cover the joins with a banding of the indigo blue cotton ribbon to form the kneebands, and finish off on the outside seams of the legs with black cotton ribbon bows.

Skirts: The closed skirts were first banded down the centre front with the deep blue felt in exactly the same width as the band down the centre front of the body, with the small black buttons continuing down to the hem. Now turn up the hem, gather the waistline evenly to the same measurement as the waistline of the body, and sew in position.

Purse, Handkerchief and Belt: First make up the purse, lining it in the same material; fold the pattern up (X to X and X to X) and oversew the sides together. Fold the purse flap downward, sewing to its centre a small black cloth-covered button. Now take two short strips of narrow grey-blue suede to suspend the purse from the waistline, sewing the bottom edges to the purse and the top edges to the waistline of the body, positioned on the right towards the side seam.

The handkerchief is a square of fine white cotton about 150mm across, hemmed all round. Position it to the left of the body and sew it in place, making sure that the top of the handkerchief will show when the belt has been added. Make up the belt in brown cotton corduroy, place it to the waistline of the body and sew in position. Now sew the arms firmly to the edge of the shoulders.

Neck Frills: Make up the two tiers in the same material as the cuffs, hemming them all round; then join and gather them together at the neck edge to fit the neckline of the figure, and sew in position.

Academic Robe: First line the two fronts with the grey cotton; then line the back of the robe and the back yoke with the black silk. Gather and sew the back to the yoke; then oversew back and front shoulder seams together, followed by oversewing the back and front side seams together.

Next, line the hanging sleeves with the black silk. Gather the heads of the sleeves so that when sewn to the armholes they terminate about 35mm down both back and front from the shoulder seams. Now oversew the sleeves into the top parts of the armholes.

Lastly, line the collar with the black silk; centre it to the centre back of the robe neckline, and oversew in position (X, X on the collar pattern indicate the fronts). Place the finished robe on the figure, and lightly catch it to either shoulder to keep it in position.

Note: hem the back skirt of the robe and its lining independently of one another.

Hat: Make up the hat, as described on page 6, in the black watered silk and add a grey felt hatband 6mm deep, at the line indicated on the pattern. Do *not* attach the hat to the head.

Head: Make up each ear in two thicknesses of the natural coloured cotton with an interlining of felt to stiffen them. Paint in the features with black dye or poster paint, and sew the completed ears to the side seams of the head. Now sew or glue the hat in position – towards the back of the head. Glue the dark brown felt moustache close to the nose, adding the red felt mouth immediately beneath it (see pattern). Carefully position the eyes of white felt *and* the dark brown felt eyebrows, slanting them down towards the top of the nose, and glue them to the face. The features – the eyes and lower lids, the cross (characterising a frown) immediately above the nose, and the bags underneath the eyes – are all painted in black.

Accessory: The clyster is made from a metal cigar container. Pierce it at each end; use epoxy glue to fix the ring end of a meat skewer into the top to form the handle, and the pointed end of a chopstick into the bottom. Paint the clyster matt grey and place it in the Doctor's hands in a menacing manner.

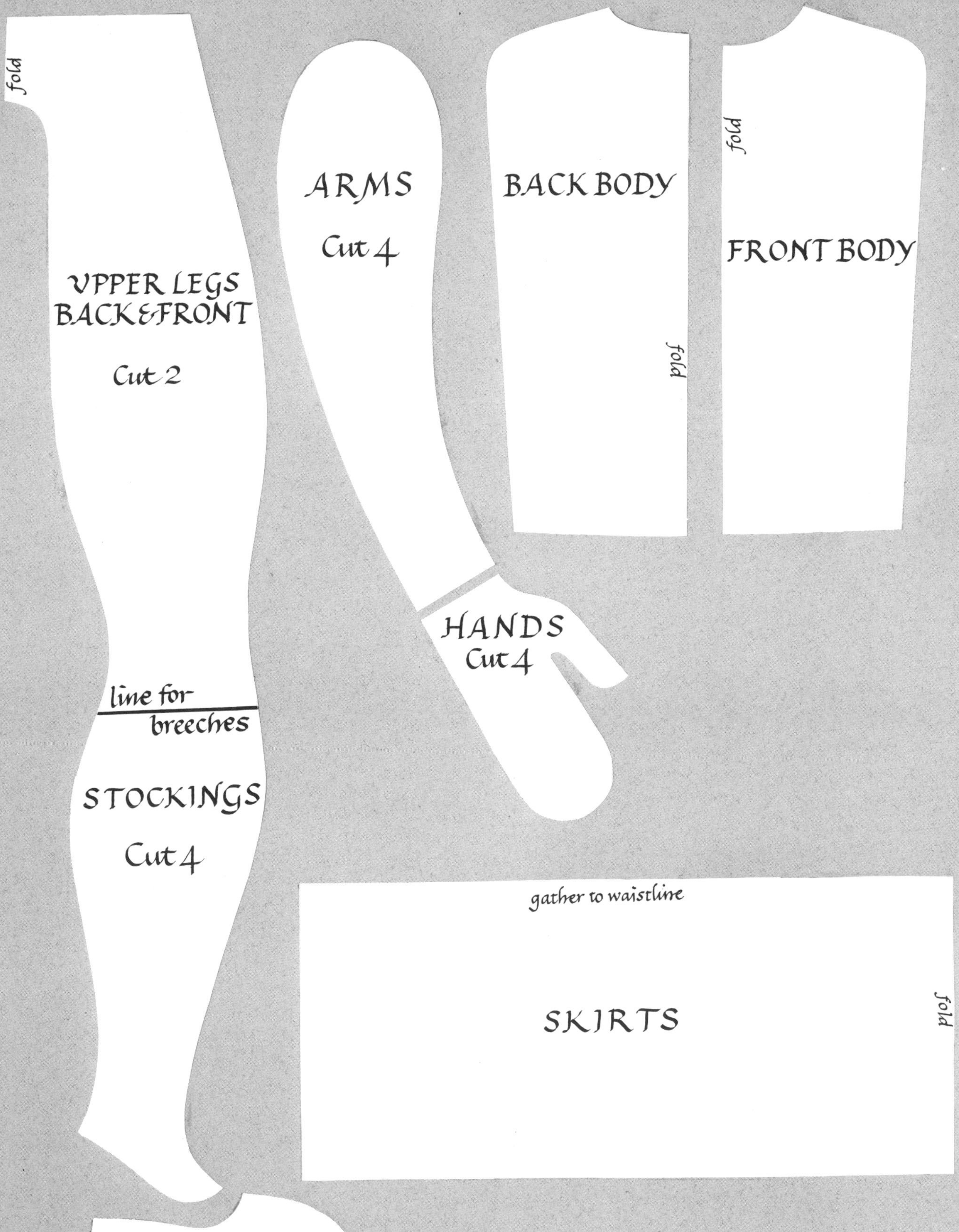

fold

UPPER LEGS
BACK & FRONT

Cut 2

ARMS

Cut 4

BACK BODY

fold

fold

FRONT BODY

line for
breeches

STOCKINGS

Cut 4

HANDS
Cut 4

gather to waistline

SKIRTS

fold

SHOES Cut 4

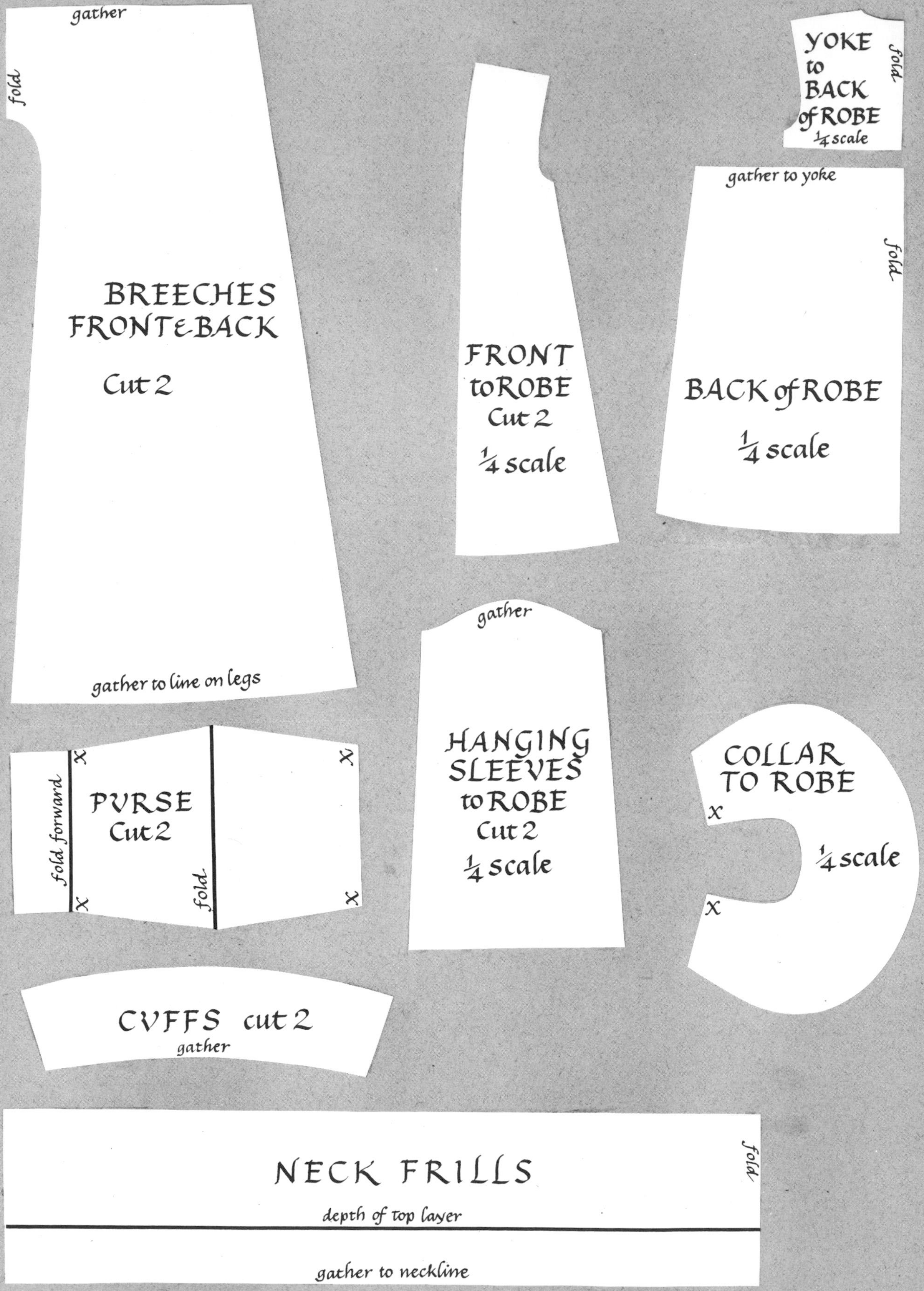

BREECHES
FRONT & BACK

Cut 2

gather

fold

gather to line on legs

FRONT to ROBE
Cut 2
$\frac{1}{4}$ scale

YOKE to BACK of ROBE
$\frac{1}{4}$ scale

fold

gather to yoke

fold

BACK of ROBE

$\frac{1}{4}$ scale

gather

HANGING SLEEVES to ROBE
Cut 2
$\frac{1}{4}$ scale

PVRSE
Cut 2

fold forward

fold

x x x x

x x

COLLAR TO ROBE

x

x

$\frac{1}{4}$ scale

CVFFS cut 2
gather

NECK FRILLS

depth of top layer

gather to neckline

fold

FRONT
TOP of FACE
Cut 2

BEARD
Cut 2

FRONT
NECK
Cut 2

MOUSTACHE

SIDES of CROWN
to HAT

position of grey hat band

SKULLCAP
BACK of HEAD

Cut 2

BACK
NECK
Cut 2

BRIM TO HAT Cut 2

TOP of
HAT

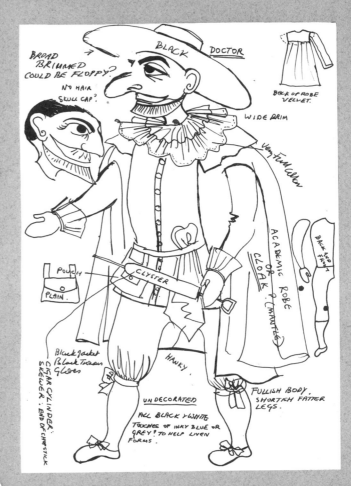

BROAD
BRIMMED
COULD BE FLOPPY?

BLACK   DOCTOR

NO HAIR
SKULL CAP.

BACK OF ROBE
VELVET.

WIDE BRIM

Very Full Collar

ACADEMIC ROBE
OR
CLOAK ? (MANTLE)

BACK AND FRONT

POUCH

PLAIN.

CLYSTER

Black Jacket
Black Trousers
Gloves

CIGAR CYLINDER
SKEWER : END OF CHOPSTICK

HANKY.

UNDECORATED

ALL BLACK Y WHITE
TOUCHES OF INKY BLUE OR
GREY ! TO HELP LIVEN
FORMS .

FULLISH BODY.
SHORTISH FATTER
LEGS.

LA BIEN-AIMÉE
Based on court fashion *c.* 1670

LA BIEN-AIMÉE

Origins and Development

Only men and boys appeared in the old Church plays, so the introduction of women into the theatre by the Italian Players was greeted with delight by the audience – especially the men. Love and love intrigues were always the central theme, and sexual encounters (often very obscene) constantly appear during most of the Commedia's history. By the second half of the seventeenth century the obscenities were replaced by more witty, amusing, and stylish dialogue and arguments based on lovers' quarrels and reconciliations. (Compare scenes between young gentlemen and ladies in the comedies of Molière and Marivaux with prints of the Italian Players depicting their encounters!)

The actress playing the Beloved was expected to be well-educated and sophisticated; many were highly talented as writers of prose, poetry, and music.

Role

The actress usually chose her own name for the role – Isabella, Flaminia, Vittoria, Rosaura. She was the adored, young and desirable daughter who refuses to accept the husband chosen for her by her father. She always gets her own way at the end of the comedy, marrying the young man of her choice and both swearing eternal love. Tougher, more manipulating and demanding than her lover, she is headstrong and determined. Men fall head-over-heels in love with her.

Character

Enchanting and elegant, her character is determined by the love entanglements and intrigues; constantly teasing and testing her lover's constancy, she is flirtatious, provocative and stubborn in turn. She generally rules her parents as well.

The Mask

She does not wear the mark, but she could carry a vizard, usually of black velvet, which was worn by all society ladies for anonymity when walking abroad to a rendezvous. The vizard had no expression, therefore it cannot truly be called a mask. It could be a simple domino covering the upper part of the face. If it was intended to hide the full face, it could be carried on a stick, tied to the head with ribbons, or kept in place by a button fastened to the inside (and uncomfortably held in the mouth).

Costume

The actress selected her own dress, always in the height of fashion, lavish in rich materials and splendid lace adorned with magnificent jewels, brooches, necklace, bracelets, hair ornaments and earrings. Sometimes, for disguise or for the *entr'actes*, she might wear a costume based on those created for the court masques (very elaborate and fancy). The actress also showed off her large wardrobe by changing her costume frequently during the action of the play. The figure in the collection is based on court costume *c.* 1670.

The bodice, cut with a low *décolletage*, is heavily boned, richly braided, the neckline edged with a flat deep fall of lace, enriched with ribbons and brooches on either shoulder; and with ribbons fanning out at the point of the long stiffened stomacher. The short, cuffed sleeves are open at the sides and reveal the chemise sleeves, full and soft, gathered in at the elbow point and terminating in falls of deep lace. Gloves cover the lower arm. The skirts, heavily enriched with bands of braiding, are pleated (bullet pleats) to fit the waist. To help 'kick' out the skirts from the waistline a small crescent-shaped pad or bolster is worn under the petticoats and skirts. Stockings can be in colour and the fronts of the shoes are elaborately decorated with ribbons and rich ornaments. The hair – parted across the front of the head and on either side above the ears – is swept up at the back, braided and coiled into a bun; sides are curled to form 'spaniel's ears' held away from the sides of the head with the help of combs. The front hair is brushed forward onto a high forehead, in a short crimped fringe. Ornaments, ribbons, jewels etc. decorate the hair. The face is painted according to the fashion of the time. A rich necklace adorns the throat and a bracelet the wrist. A large folding fan imported from the East is a very valuable and fashionable addition to the toilette.

The costume must be worn with bravura – it was heavy and greatly restricted natural body movements – needing great assurance to show it off with ease and confidence.

Movement

Always accomplished in the art of dancing, with the elegance, etiquette and style demanded by court conventions.

Speech, Voice and Other Skills

Originally the language was Tuscan, but in Paris the actresses soon adopted, and spoke in, French. The Beloved was never at a loss for well-phrased language, even at the height of a violent quarrel, argument or lament. An accomplished singer, capable as a musician and playing various instruments, the actress was recommended to read good authors and poets. She must be beautiful, eloquent and amusing. Actresses frequently played this role until they were quite old, as many international ballerinas (and French actresses) do today, before relinquishing the part to someone somewhat younger; the *essence* of enchantment was required, not *naturalism*.

Materials

There is no restriction of colour or material in making this figure, but the final result should be rich and handsome.

Cotton: natural colour (head and shoulders, nose, legs, hip bolster, foundation for chemise and top cuffed sleeves)
Felt: ginger (fullness back of head, bun foundation, basis for hair)
    white (eyes)
Silk: brown heavy silk (shoes)
    patterned or striped silk (body, cuffed sleeves)
    brown soft silk or brushed nylon (skirts)
    red (petticoat)
    orange (arms)
    natural coloured soft silk (chemise sleeves)
    pale pink (cuffs, banding on skirts)
Velvet: orange (stomacher)

Ribbons: cherry-red velvet (cuffs, stomacher, body, hair orna-
ments) 6mm and 12mm
pink (body, stomacher, chemise sleeves) 6mm
brown (body) 20mm
beige (cuffed sleeves, skirts) 12mm and 6mm
embroidered or woven patterned (skirts, stomacher)
about 35mm
Lace: off white (chemise sleeves, neckline) 35mm to 40mm
Braid: brown Russian (shoes)
Cord: gold (shoe ties)
Jute: hair (dyed deep pink through to auburn)
Two handsome buttons or brooches: (shoes)
Two handsome brooches: (shoulders)
A fine jewelled ornament: (top of bun)
Beads and pearls: (wrist, bun, hair ornaments)
Collection of jewels: (necklace)
Dyes: pink (mouth)
black (face features)
green and grey (eyelids, eyes)
Card: (stomacher)
Padding

Making

Basic Figure: Braid front and back body parts, following the
patterns, in the pink ribbon; add the band of brown ribbon
down the centre back. Assemble and sew all front and all back
sections together. Sew completed front body to completed back
body, turn right side out and pad. Cover side seams of the
bodice with the 12mm cherry-red velvet ribbons. Edge the top
of the shoes with brown Russian braid, placing little gold cord
bows and a button or rich ornament to the fronts.

The added fullness at the back of the head is of felt (centre
back placed at X as shown on pattern), eased and gathered
around the side seams of the head, sewn in position and padded
with cottonwool to achieve the necessary shape.

Skirts and Petticoats: Hem petticoats top and bottom; gather
and sew the top edge to the waistline of the figure. Hem skirts
top and bottom; and richly braid down the front and around
the hem. Bullet pleat (or closely gather) the top edge and sew to
the waistline – over the petticoats – allowing the bulk of the
pleating to commence 20mm on either side of the centre front
and effectively display the braiding.

Make up bolster and pad; place it underneath the petticoats,
centring it to the centre back of the figure, and sew to just below
the waistline.

Arms and Sleeves: Sew up arms, turn and pad. Make up
chemise sleeves first by sewing gathered lace to the lower edges
(X to X on pattern); then sew up the side seams. Gather heads
of sleeves and the line where the lace is to be joined, to the same
measurements as the foundation. Join up the side seams of the
foundation and mount the chemise sleeves to them. Position on
the arms, firmly sew and gather the edge to the line marked on
the arm pattern. Now cover the line of gathering with pink

ribbon terminating in a bow on the inside or outside of the
sleeves. Firmly sew the arms to the edge of the shoulders.
Lastly, gather and sew the heads of the chemise sleeves to the
body, following a natural line to simulate the armholes.

The cuffed sleeves are made similarly. They should be mounted
and gathered, top and bottom edges, to the foundations – with
the outside openings and heads bound in 6mm deep beige
ribbon. The pink silk cuffs, lined with the same material, are
trimmed with cherry-red velvet ribbon terminating in a bow.
Oversew the cuffs to the lower edges of the sleeves. Now place
on the arms and sew the heads of the finished sleeves to the
body following the line of the armholes formed by the chemise
sleeves. Lastly, puff out the chemise sleeves through the outside
openings of the cuffed sleeves.

Stomacher and Additional Trimmings: Cut the stomacher
from card and cover with orange velvet. Richly braid the centre
front and edge all round with the pink ribbon. At the base of the
point, sew in a 'fan' of loops of red velvet and pink ribbons.
Firmly glue the finished stomacher to the centre front of the
bodice, positioning it to the edge of the bodice neckline.

The lace collar is darted at regular intervals, and when
completed forms a deep curve following the shape of the neckline of the bodice. Sew in position and edge with a narrow band
of the pink ribbon. On either shoulder place a fine bow of fancy
red ribbon centred with a brooch or ornament.

Hair and Ornaments: Begin by tightly placing together and
glueing loops of jute to the strips of felt; cut the ends of the loops,
unravelling the jute to create curls. Giving a high forehead, sew
or glue the fringe in position. Following the hair-style, glue the
jute across the top of the head, making sure to cover the top felt
edge of the fringe. Continue to apply the jute down the back
and sides of the head. Now make up the bun foundation in felt
and cover it completely with a plait of tightly woven jute; pack
with cottonwool and sew it high to the back of the head. Next
sew or glue the 'spaniel's ears' to the sides of the head, trimming
the length and thinning out the under sections of the curls.

Decorate the join of the side curls to the head with elaborate
bows of red velvet ribbon and with loops of beads and pearls.
The bun could also be enriched with strings of beads around its
sides and a fine jewelled ornament placed on the top.

Face: Make up the nose, pad with soft cottonwool, and sew in
position. Paint the mouth in pink, with the smile and chin
drawn in black. The eyes of felt are painted green and the
eyelids in black, tinted with tones of green and grey. The eyes
should be angled to give a provocative look when glued to the
head. Lastly, paint in the arched eyebrows immediately above
the upper eyelids.

Accessories: A bracelet, a fine necklace (you must use invention here supported with research), and an open fan glued to
the hand. (The fan can usually be bought at a Chinese 'gift'
shop and cut to scale.)

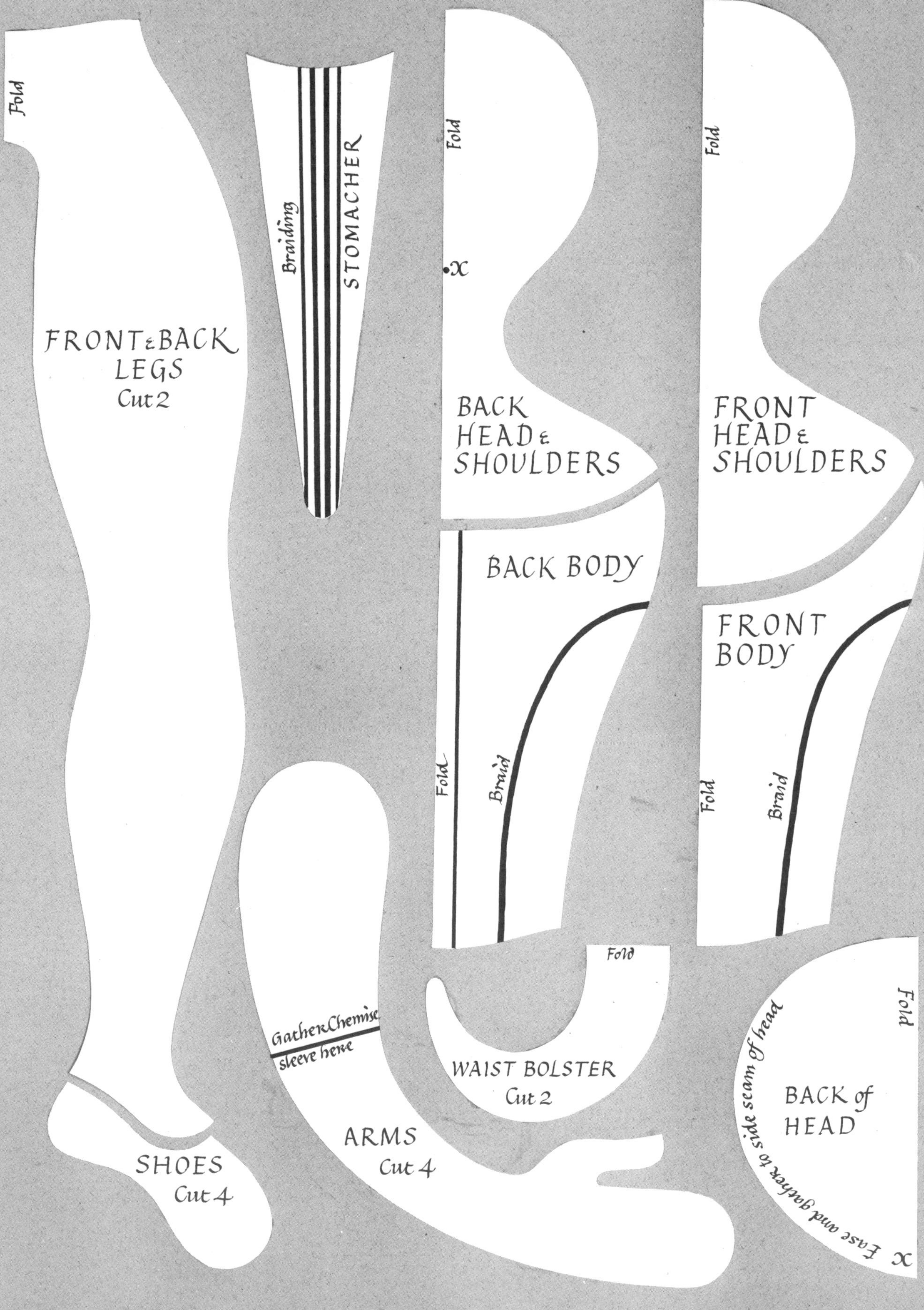

FRONT & BACK
LEGS
Cut 2

Fold

Braiding

STOMACHER

Fold

• X

BACK
HEAD &
SHOULDERS

BACK BODY

Fold

Braid

FRONT
HEAD &
SHOULDERS

FRONT
BODY

Fold

Braid

Fold

Gather Chemise
sleeve here

WAIST BOLSTER
Cut 2

ARMS
Cut 4

SHOES
Cut 4

Fold

BACK of
HEAD

X Ease and gather to side seam of head

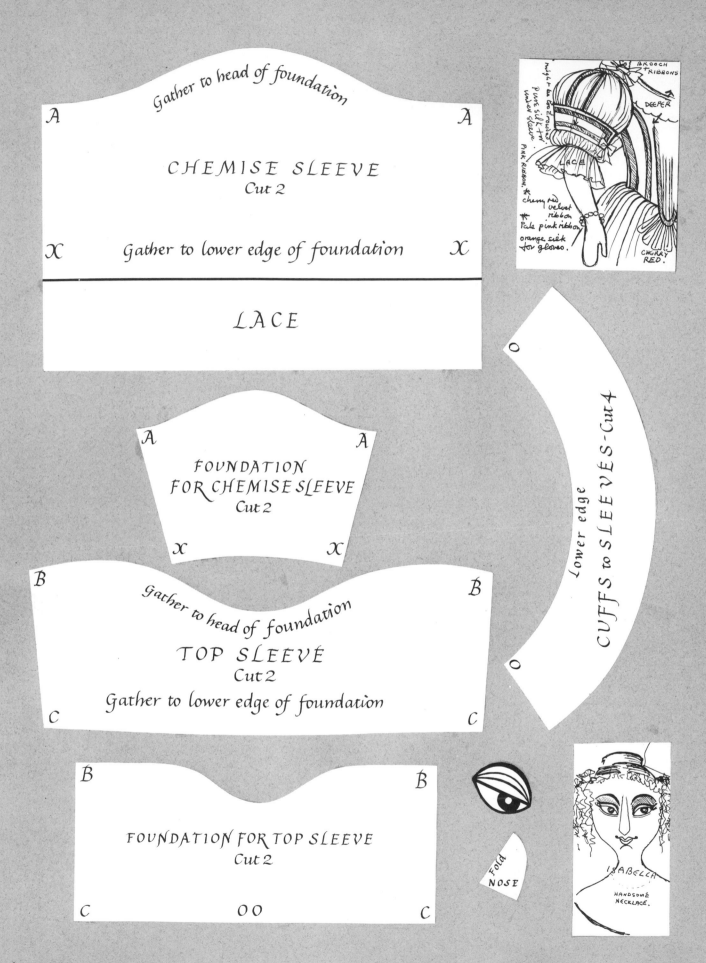

CHEMISE SLEEVE
Cut 2

Gather to head of foundation

A   A

X   Gather to lower edge of foundation   X

LACE

FOUNDATION
FOR CHEMISE SLEEVE
Cut 2

A   A

X   X

TOP SLEEVE
Cut 2

Gather to head of foundation

B   B

Gather to lower edge of foundation

C   C

FOUNDATION FOR TOP SLEEVE
Cut 2

B   B

C   OO   C

O

O

Lower edge

CUFFS to SLEEVES - Cut 4

Fold
NOSE

ISABELLA

HANDSOME NECKLACE.

BROOCH RIBBONS

DEEPER

LACE

PINK RIBBON

might be too small for pure silk for under sleeve.

cherry red velvet ribbon
Pale pink ribbon
orange silk for gloves.

CHERRY RED.

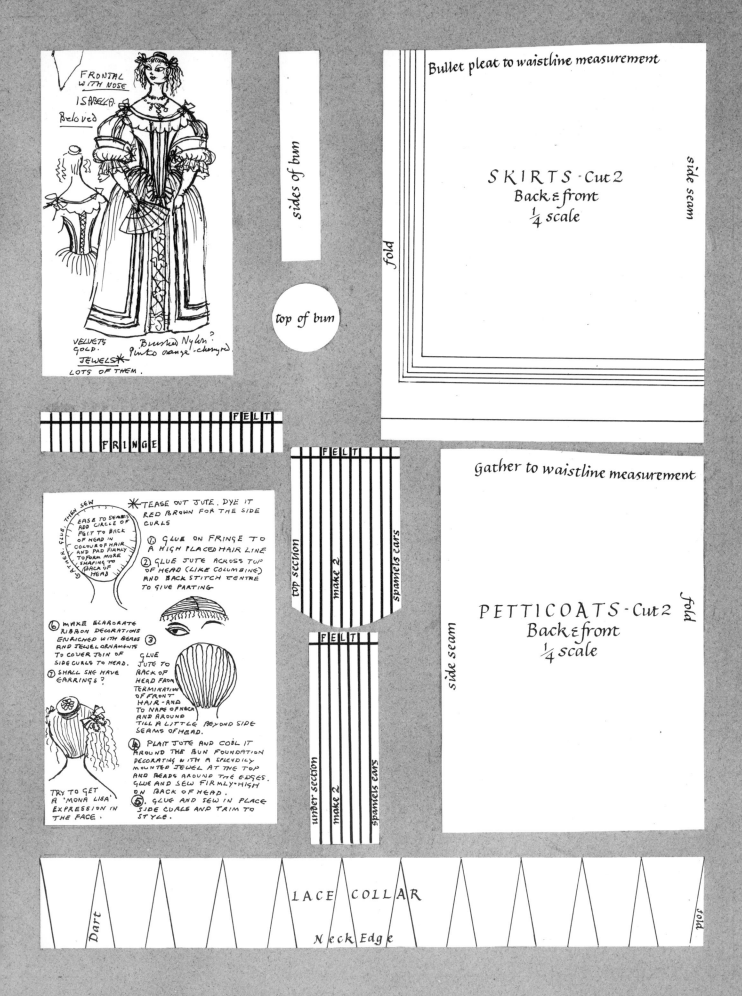

FRONTAL WITH NOSE

ISABELLA

Beloved

VELVETS GOLD. Brushed Nylon? Pinto orange. cherry red.

JEWELS* LOTS OF THEM.

FRINGE — FELT

*TEASE OUT JUTE. DYE IT RED BROWN FOR THE SIDE CURLS

① GLUE ON FRINGE TO A HIGH PLACED HAIR LINE

② GLUE JUTE ACROSS TOP OF HEAD (LIKE COLUMBINE) AND BACK STITCH CENTRE TO GIVE PARTING

GATHER, GLUE, THEN SEW. EASE TO SEAMS ADD CIRCLE OF FELT TO BACK OF HEAD IN COLOUR OF HAIR AND PAD FIRMLY TO FORM MORE SHAPING TO BACK OF HEAD

③ GLUE JUTE TO BACK OF HEAD FROM TERMINATION OF FRONT HAIR - AND TO NAPE OF NECK AND AROUND TILL A LITTLE BEYOND SIDE SEAMS OF HEAD.

④ PLAIT JUTE AND COIL IT AROUND THE BUN FOUNDATION DECORATING WITH A SPLENDILY MOUNTED JEWEL AT THE TOP AND BEADS AROUND THE EDGES. GLUE AND SEW FIRMLY. HIGH ON BACK OF HEAD.

⑤ GLUE AND SEW IN PLACE SIDE CURLS AND TRIM TO STYLE.

⑥ MAKE ELABORATE RIBBON DECORATIONS ENRICHED WITH BEADS AND JEWEL ORNAMENTS TO COVER JOIN OF SIDE CURLS TO HEAD.

⑦ SHALL SHE HAVE EARRINGS?

TRY TO GET A 'MONA LISA' EXPRESSION IN THE FACE.

sides of bun

top of bun

top section — FELT — make 2 — spaniels ears

under section — FELT — make 2 — spaniels ears

Bullet pleat to waistline measurement

SKIRTS · Cut 2
Back & front
¼ scale

fold

side seam

Gather to waistline measurement

PETTICOATS · Cut 2
Back & front
¼ scale

side seam

fold

LACE COLLAR

Neck Edge

Dart

fold

L'AMANT

Based on contemporary costume *c.* 1660-1670

44

L'AMANT

Origins and Development

Many of the plays of Terence and Plautus, and the medieval Romances, have as their story-line the conflict of love, youth and old age. This theme regularly appears in the Italian Comedy. Most audiences enjoy seeing youth painfully and stubbornly involved in a first great love-encounter, following the passions, pains, fears and jealousies of the situation. The lover in the Commedia can be very clearly identified in the plays of Molière and in the comedies and romantic plays of Shakespeare.

Role

The actor usually chose his own name for the role – Leandro, Flavio, Fabrizio, Ottavio, amongst others. He was played as a young gentleman or soldier of good breeding. Enchanting, attractive, and very jealous, he pursues the young girl on whom his ardour is centred – though he is not averse to having a flirtation with her maid or lady-in-waiting, or even an affair with a young courtesan.

He is vain, petulant, doubting, emotional and lacking in patience. He frequently invents a quarrel to test his beloved's constancy. There are many partings, and reconciliations usually resolved with the help and/or common sense of the male and female servants. The lovers are the mainspring of the plot in most Commedia scenarios, though their roles may appear dull and ordinary compared to the bizarre characterisations of Arlequin, le Médecin, Pantalone etc.

The Mask

The lover never wears a mask, unless for disguise.

Costume

He is usually dressed as a young soldier or cadet. The figure in the collection is based on French costume c. 1660-1670. He wears the typical high-waisted and skirted coat with belt. The join of the sleeves and the false hanging sleeves to the shoulders are concealed by elaborately braided shoulder rolls, finished off on the outside edge with loops of pink ribbons. The sleeves terminate in upstanding starched cuffs edged with deep lace. The falling collar, tied high at the throat, is also edged with lace. The open breeches terminate in deep bands of pink ribbon loops and bows. A mid-thigh-length semicircular collared cloak and elaborately fringed gauntlet gloves could also be worn. The entire costume is richly braided. He carries his sword in a hanger or baldrick suspended from his right shoulder across his chest. Instead of stockings and buckled shoes he could wear elegant knee-length 'bucket boots', meeting the breeches, the cups filled inside with deep gatherings of lace (see Crispin's boots, p. 88).

The hair is curled and shoulder-length, and he wears fashionable small pointed moustaches and Imperial beard. The hat (regular attire for any gentleman, or soldier) is flamboyantly decorated with a large sweeping cockade of mixed feathers arranged around the inside of the wide, upturned brim.

Movement

The actor had to have been taught excellent deportment and grace of movement, to be very polite in manner, and know all the necessary formalities of court behaviour. He must also be a capable swordsman.

Speech, Voice and Other Skills

The language was originally Tuscan, but by the end of the seventeenth century in Paris the Lover spoke in French. Elaborately embellished, the words are elegantly chosen and beautifully spoken – at times *too* flowery. He speaks poetry, and the voice was trained to be musical in contrast to the rougher accents of so many of the other characters. The actor playing the lover needed to have a good and thorough classical education and be able to improvise his own love-poetry and soliloquies. His passionate and often violent love scenes were played with virtuosity, panache and accurate timing – such scenes were frequently not improvised but carefully rehearsed. He sings and dances, and can accompany himself on a variety of stringed instruments.

Materials

There is no restriction of colour or material in making this figure, but try to echo the colour scheme of the Beloved.

Cotton: natural colour (head, nose, hands, upper part of legs)
    navy blue (shoulder rolls, hanging sleeve linings)
Cotton velvet: brown strips (breeches) 20mm
Silk: small-patterned in blue and orange (body, arms, skirts, breeches)
    peach (stockings)
    beige (shoes)
    chocolate (hanging sleeves, skirt lining)
    tangerine (belt, sword hanger)
    deep orange (hat)
Ribbon: a variety of braids and ribbons will be needed to decorate the entire costume – (browns, beige, pinks). Specifically:
    pink (shoulder rolls, breeches, hat) 6mm, 12mm
    brown, and ribbed silk (body) 12mm
    white (neckline, wrists) 12mm
    dark blue (shoes) 12mm
Braid: brown Russian (shoes)
Lawn: white (collar)
Lace: white (cuffs)
    white (collar) 10mm
Felt: brown (basis for hair, eyebrows, moustaches, beard)
    white (eyes)
Jute: brown (hair)
Gold buttons: (body)
Two handsome ornaments: (shoes)
Buckle: (belt)
Splendid variety of feathers: (hat)
Dyes: black, blue and pink (face features)
Card: (hat)
Padding

Making

Basic Figure: Sew a 12mm band of pink ribbon down the centre front of the body, covering the edges first with a narrow band of brown ribbon, then a wider band of ribbed brown silk ribbon; gold buttons are set at regular intervals down the centre front. Now assemble and sew all front and all back sections together and sew the completed front body to the completed back body; turn right side out and pad. Edge the tops of the shoes with the brown Russian braid, and decorate the fronts with bows of dark blue ribbon centred with a handsome buckle or ornament.

Assemble, make up and pad the arms, adding the darted lace cuffs to the wrists, banded with white cotton ribbon to cover the join. Do *not* attach the arms to the body.

Open Breeches: Lavishly decorate both the full length of the front and the back of the breeches with a variety of ribbons and braids. Sew the front to the back and edge the hems of the leg openings with two bands of contrasting brown ribbon, set one above the other. Now, at the base of the bands, add loops of the narrow pink ribbon, 25mm deep, set closely together all round. Finish off on the outside of each leg with a double bow of brown ribbon.

The breeches can now be placed on the figure. Gather and sew the waistline of the breeches to the waistline of the body. Make sure that the side seams of the breeches correspond with the side seams of the body.

Skirts: Line the skirts with the chocolate-brown silk. Edge down the fronts and around the hem with brown silk ribbon, adding a band of pink ribbon to the inside edges of the brown ribbon at the fronts. Sew the top of the skirts to the join of breeches to body.

Belt: The waistline is finished off with a belt of tangerine-coloured silk complete with buckle. (When placing the belt follow the line as indicated on the patterns.)

Arms, Hanging Sleeves and Shoulder Rolls: Now sew the arms firmly to the edge of the shoulders. Follow this by making up the hanging sleeves in chocolate-brown silk, lined with navy-blue cotton. Down the sides and hem of the brown side of the sleeves edge with the 12mm pink ribbon. Gather the heads of the sleeves to 75mm and firmly sew them over the join of arms to shoulders. Make sure that they are centrally balanced to the shoulder seams before sewing.

The shoulder rolls, of navy-blue cotton, are each made up in two thicknesses of the material, turned right side out and padded with soft cottonwool. Decorate with bands of the 6mm pink ribbon, set at regular intervals, around the circumference. Add loops of the pink ribbon, echoing the loops around the edges of the breeches, to the outside edges of the rolls. Balance the finished rolls centrally to the end of the shoulder seams, and sew them very firmly to the body; the ends of the rolls should almost meet under the arms.

Collar: Make up the collar in white lawn, lining it with the same material, and edge all round (save the neckline) with lace. Fold the two front edges of the collar to the front (see pattern) and, easing the neckline to fit the line of the join of head to body, sew in position. Cover this join with a band of the white cotton ribbon, adding a bow of the same ribbon high to the centre front.

Hat: The making of the hat should follow, with minor exceptions, the instructions on p. 6. Make up the crown first, followed by the brim – all in the deep orange silk. The sides of the brim are *not* sewn together but left open. Place the upturned brim to the base of the crown, with the open sides of the brim positioned well back from the left-hand side of the head, then closely oversew it to the crown.

Now edge the top and sides of the brim, 12mm down, with the narrow pink ribbon. Lastly, decorate the inside of the brim with a swirl of feathers, using as many different types of feathers as you can find to harmonize with the general colour-scheme of the dress. Do not sew or glue the hat to the head until the hair and the nose have been completed.

Head: First make up the three sections for the hair, using the same process as described on p. 10 (Molière), but glue or sew the fringe lower down on the forehead. Then make up the nose, pad it with soft cottonwool, and sew in position. The hat can now be firmly fixed to the head.

Position the eyes of white felt and glue them to the face; do the same with the brown felt eyebrows and with the moustache, which should only be glued at its centre immediately under the nose. Next, with pink, paint in the mouth with a fine black line for the smile. The little brown felt Imperial beard is glued only at the top, and positioned immediately below the mouth. Lastly outline the upper eyelids with black and paint the pupils blue.

Sword Hanger: Make up in the tangerine-coloured silk, lining it with the same material. Join up the base and decorate it, some 60mm up both back and front, with braid. Back-stitch the front and back together 12mm up from the base, to form a slot to hold the sword. Now it can be placed on the figure, across the chest and over the right shoulder.

Sword: The sword is made from a chopstick, adding a handsome knob for the pommel; and the guard from a large piece of costume jewellery in the shape of a Tudor rose. (If something like this cannot be obtained, then, using imagination, make up the pommel and guard in gold card paper sculpture.) Use epoxy glue to stick the parts together, and place the sword in its hanger.

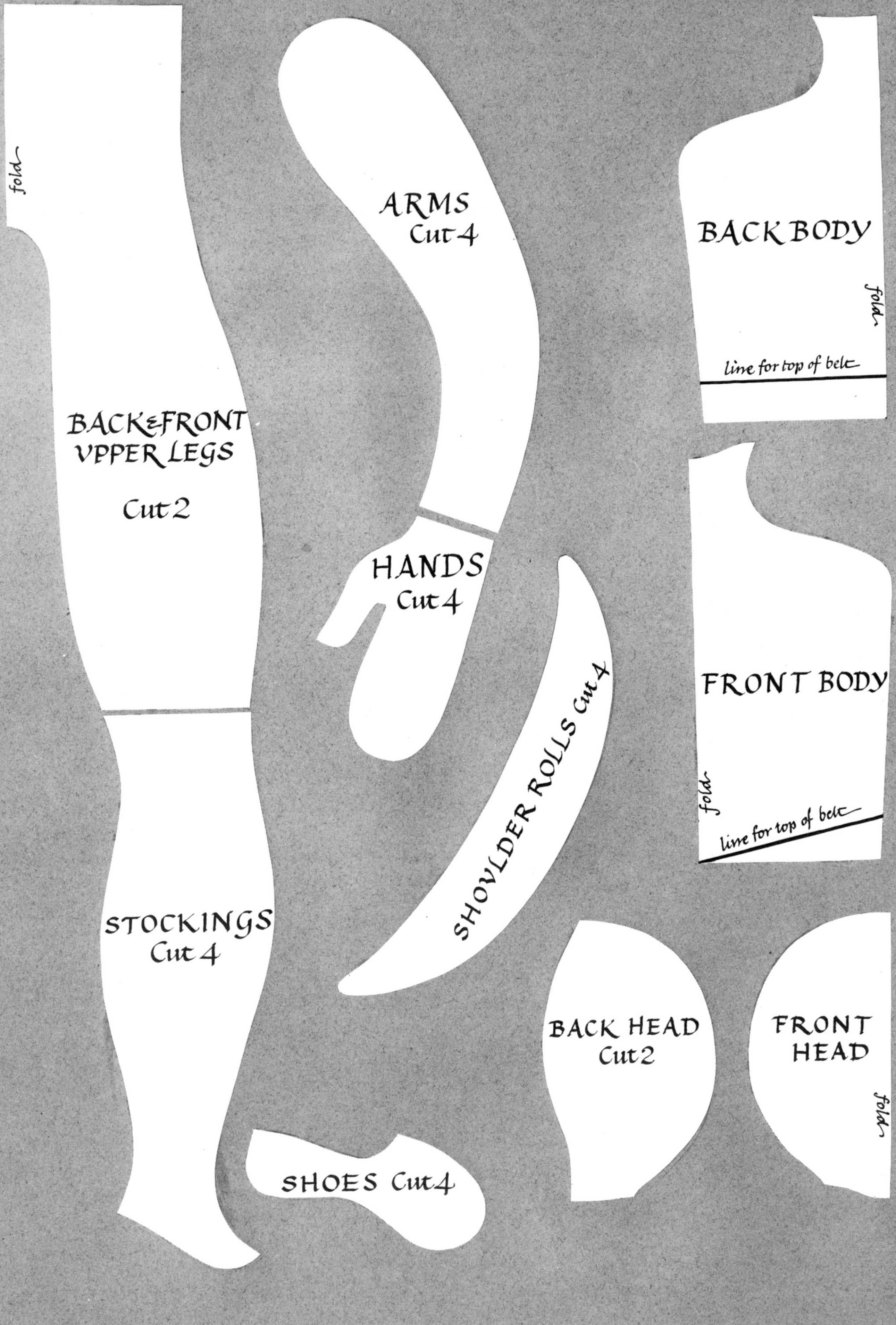

ARMS
Cut 4

BACK BODY
fold
line for top of belt

BACK&FRONT
VPPER LEGS
Cut 2

fold

HANDS
Cut 4

FRONT BODY
fold
line for top of belt

SHOVLDER ROLLS Cut 4

STOCKINGS
Cut 4

BACK HEAD
Cut 2

FRONT
HEAD
fold

SHOES Cut 4

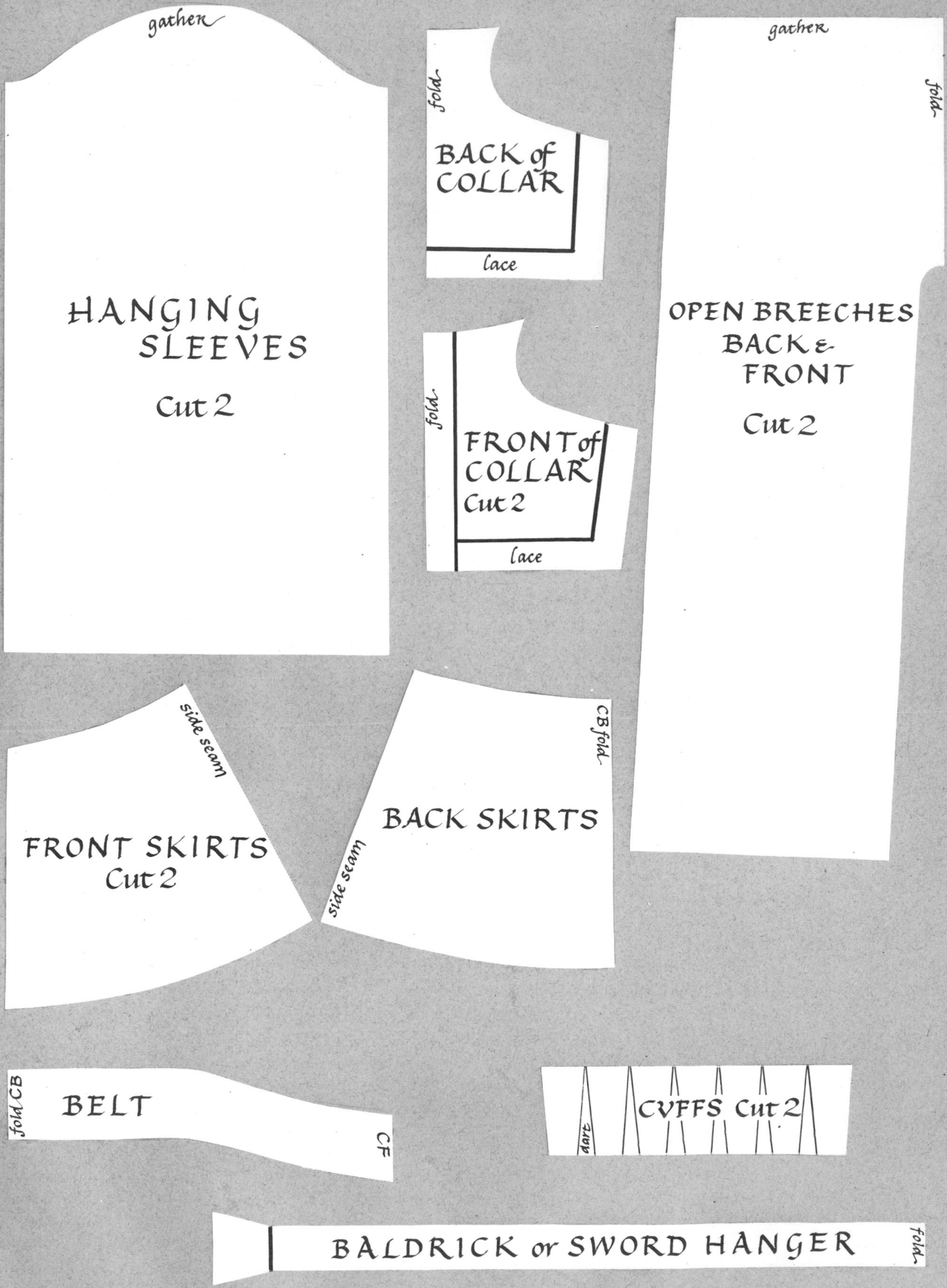

gather

fold

**BACK of
COLLAR**

lace

gather

fold

**HANGING
SLEEVES**

Cut 2

fold

**FRONT of
COLLAR
Cut 2**

lace

**OPEN BREECHES
BACK &
FRONT**

Cut 2

side seam

CB fold

**FRONT SKIRTS
Cut 2**

BACK SKIRTS

side seam

side seam

fold CB

BELT

CF

dart

CVFFS Cut 2

BALDRICK or SWORD HANGER

fold

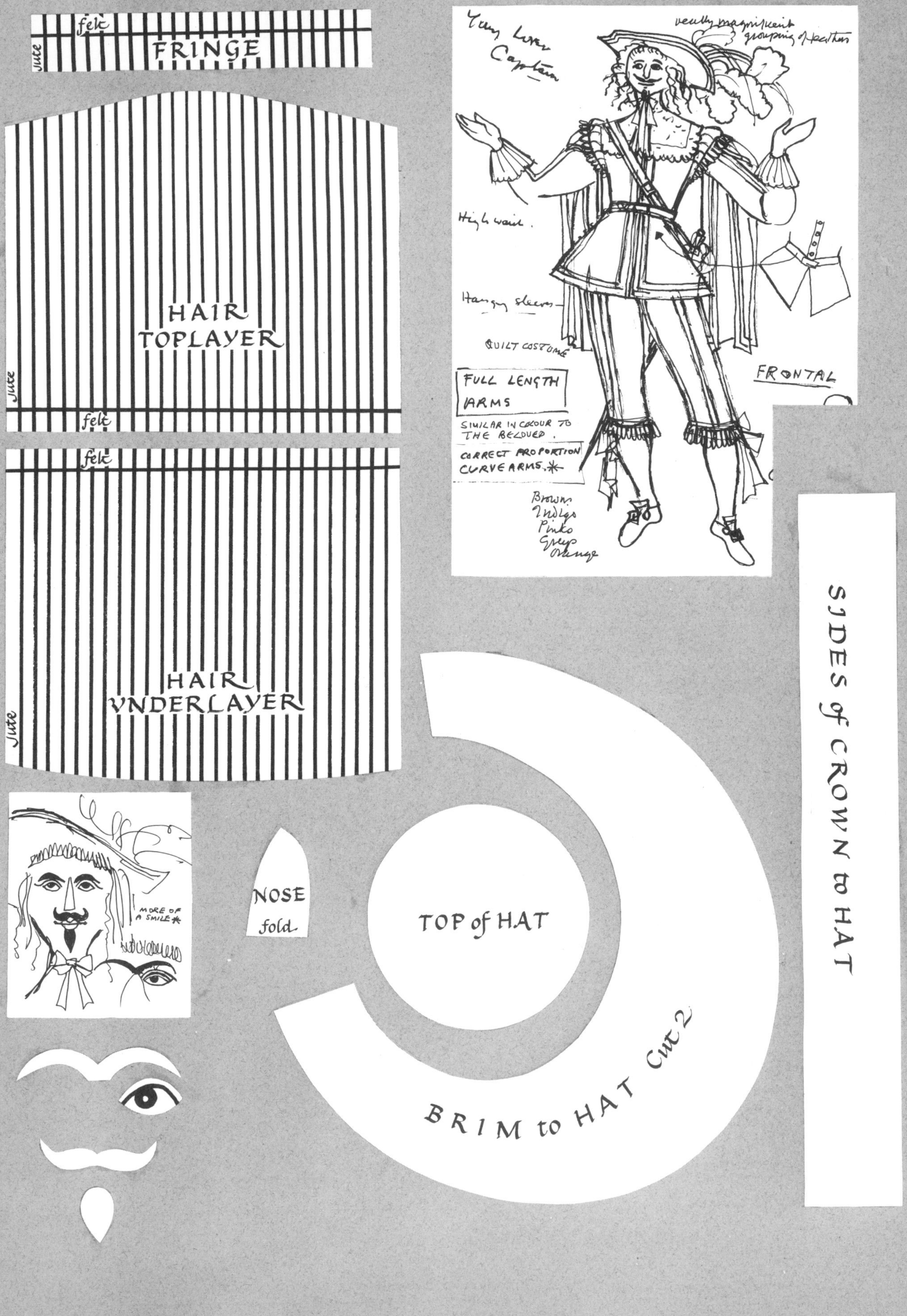

FRINGE
jute felt

HAIR
TOPLAYER
jute
felt

HAIR
VNDERLAYER
felt
Jute

Young Lovers
Captain

vendy magnificent
grouping of feathers

High waist.

Hangy sleeves

QUILT COSTUME

FULL LENGTH
ARMS

SIMILAR IN COLOUR TO
THE BELOVED.

CORRECT PROPORTION
CURVE ARMS. *

FRONTAL

Browns
Indigo
Pinks
Greys
Orange

MORE OF
A SMILE *

NOSE
fold

TOP of HAT

SIDES of CROWN to HAT

BRIM to HAT Cut 2

COLUMBINE
Conjectural *c.* 1700

50

COLVMBINE

Origins and Development

A *servetta – zagne* (Italian or *servette* (French) – Columbine is a typical soubrette role. Later examples can be seen in practically every operetta and certainly in Mozart's Susanna (*Marriage of Figaro*), and Despina (*Così fan tutte*). When women first appeared on the stage in the Commedia in the sixteenth century there were few roles for them to play, but by the end of the seventeenth century young women were appearing in profusion (though often only in the *entr'actes*), to enchant their audiences with singing and dancing. We might call them the forerunners of today's 'show girls' or ladies of the chorus. Some, however, were given very important roles, like Columbine, who was usually the personal maid or lady-in-waiting to a family and who particularly acted as *confidante* to the daughter(s).

Columbine often had assistant or 'secondary' maids, who were dressed in white, wearing aprons and little caps or kerchiefs.

Role

A maid, usually accompanied by a male servant companion/lover whom she often marries at the end of the comedy. She helps the young lovers, with the assistance of her boy-friend, in arranging secret assignations and meetings for them, generally being paid for her work. Often, to add to the humour of the plot, she is not averse to muddling situations up on purpose. Both Molière and Shakespeare frequently introduce these characteristics in their senior maids, as for example Nicola in *le Bourgeois gentilhomme* and Maria in *Twelfth Night*.

Character

Cheeky, fearless, often sharp and malicious in wit; petite and full of gaiety and charm, she coquettes the male servants as well as sometimes flirting with their masters. Columbine parodied the courtly love and behaviour of the time. A very famous and successful interpreter of this role was Caterina Biancolelli, who was born in Paris, first appearing on the stage there in 1683. She was the daughter of Doménique, the famous Harlequin. Like the Beloved, the actress often chose her own name for the character. 'Camille' was a favourite, but Columbine remained universal, and is still associated with the Commedia through ballets based on the Harlequinade.

The Mask

The mask is not worn, save for the occasional wearing of the domino. The actress must appear pretty, enchanting and attractive according to the conventions of the time.

Costume

It is sometimes very difficult to distinguish the ladies from their maids, due to the elaborate dress the more senior female servants wore. The skirts, however, were usually cut short, without a train, to permit greater freedom for dancing. When companion, mistress, or wife to Harlequin she was called Harlequine – wearing a costume identical in design to that of Harlequin except that she wore skirts and not trousers (though there is a print showing her, in disguise, dressed entirely in the Harlequin costume).

The character as interpreted in soft sculpture is based on pseudo-country or pastoral style in contrast to the court costume worn by the Beloved. She wears a heavily corseted bodice with a boned and laced stomacher ending in a deep point. The neckline is cut low. The sleeves finish at elbow-point from which fall deep lace frills. Lace also finishes off the neckline with the addition of an edging of pearls. The neck, wrist and hair ornaments too are of pearls.

The full skirts, with a top deep basque skirt in the same material as the bodice, are bullet-pleated to the waistline. They are ankle length and held out by one or more petticoats. The shoes are soft with ribbon ties echoing the general colour-scheme of the costume – beige, honey, yellow, white, soft greens, blue and gold. A narrow embroidered white apron terminates under the point of the stomacher with a fan of white lace. Her hair is blonde and is dressed and decorated in the same fashion as the Beloved – though shorter and less finely curled. She can wear a cap with lappets or a kerchief tied under the chin.

Movement

An excellent mimic – often appearing in disguise – she must be nimble and fast in her actions – running, butting in, and then quickly making her escape. She is also very flirtatious.

Speech, Voice and Other Skills

In France the maids alternated much of their dialogue with a mixture of Italian, sometimes in dialect, and French. They have a sharp tongue, stinging as a wasp, and their language is laced with a barbed sense of wit. The actress had to possess a pleasing speaking and singing voice, be a capable musician, and dance well.

Materials

There is no restriction of colour or materials in the making of this figure, but the final result should be delicate and feminine.

Cotton: natural colour (head, neck and chest, lower arms, nose)
       grey (basque skirt lining)
Silk: soft green patterned (body, upper arms, basque skirt)
    dark green (legs)
    brown (shoes)
    bright green (petticoats)
    beige (skirts)
    primrose yellow (skirts)
    cream (skirts)
    grey (stomacher)
Ribbon: antique brocade in blue and gold (skirt) 35mm
    beige (body, upper arms, basque skirt, stomacher) 6mm
    indigo (arms) 12mm
    yellow (shoes) 10mm
    pale blue (shoes) 10mm
    dark blue (stomacher, shoes) 6mm
    royal blue (head) 12mm
    white (head) 15mm
Lace: white (arms, neckline, stomacher point) about 45mm

Lurex: white patterned silver (apron)
Braid: yellow Russian (shoes)
  brown (back body)
Felt: yellow (back of head, bun foundation, basis for hair, stomacher lining)
  white (eyes)
Jute: yellow (hair)
Pearls: (neckline, neck, wrists, hair ornaments)
Dyes: blue, black and pink (face features)
Card: grey (stomacher)
Padding

Making

Basic Figure: Braid the two curved simulated seams with the beige ribbon, and the centre back with a band of the brown braid as shown on the back body. Assemble and sew all back and all front sections together. Sew completed front body to completed back body; turn right side out and pad.

Edge the top of the shoes with the yellow Russian braid, placing neat bows of yellow, pale and dark blue ribbons to the fronts.

The added fullness at the back of the head is of yellow felt and padded following the same instructions as those for la Bien-Aimée (see p. 40).

Assemble, make up and pad the arms, covering the side seams of the upper arms with the narrow beige ribbon. Add deep frills of gathered white lace to the join of upper arms to lower arms and cover the joins with a 12mm band of the indigo blue ribbon. The arms are now complete, but do *not* attach them to the body.

Skirts, Petticoat, Basque Skirt, and Apron: First gather and hem the petticoat and sew it to the waistline. Do the same with the skirts (use three different coloured silks of equal depth to make the skirt, starting with cream at the top, followed by primrose yellow, with the last width in beige adding a deep band of antique brocade ribbon to cover this seam). The skirts when gathered to the waistline of the figure should terminate above the ankles.

Next hem and make up the apron, of white and silver Lurex. Gather the top edge to a width of 50mm and sew it to the centre front of the body waistline; add a fan of deep white lace to cover this join.

The Basque skirt, made up in the same material as the body and the upper arms, is lined with grey cotton. Now add a band of the narrow beige ribbon, down the fronts and around the hem, placing it 12mm up from the edges of the finished skirt. Then sew the waist edge to the figure (it may require a little easing) covering the join of the skirts proper to the body waistline. The Basque skirts should *not* meet at the centre front – allow a gap of 30mm.

Stomacher: Make up in grey silk (lined with felt), applying narrow bands of the dark blue ribbon, set at regular intervals, across the finished shape. Now glue to the back of the base of the stomacher a piece of card, to terminate some 60mm up. Sew the finished stomacher to the centre front of the body, positioning it to commence at the edge of the bodice neckline.

Braiding: The sides and point of the stomacher and the join of skirts to waistline are all edged with the narrow beige ribbon.

Neckline: Gather a length of the same white lace as used for the sleeve frills 12mm down from the top edge, to the same measurement as the body neckline; then sew in position and cover this sewing line with a string of pearls set very closely together. Now sew the arms firmly to the edge of the shoulders.

Hair and Ornaments: Follow the directions for the placing and making of the hair as described for la Bien-Aimée on p. 40. The final result should not appear so elegant or carefully coiffeured – the side hair is shorter and thicker and the fringe is less delicately crimped.

Decorate the join of the side curls to the head with double bows of white satin and blue ribbon, and with short loops of pearls. Finish off around the base of the bun with a single string of pearls.

Face: Make up the nose, pad it with soft cottonwool, and sew it in position to give a saucy and cheeky expression (*retroussé*). Now glue the white felt eyes to the face. All the features should then be added with dye or poster paint: a pink mouth, with a strong cupid's bow upper lip, outlined in black; black also for the chin and fine highly-placed eyebrows; black outlines the upper eyelids and the pupils glance to the side in blue.

Accessories: Three strings of pearls at the wrist and three to form the necklace. To complete the sculpture place a small mauve/pink rose in her left hand.

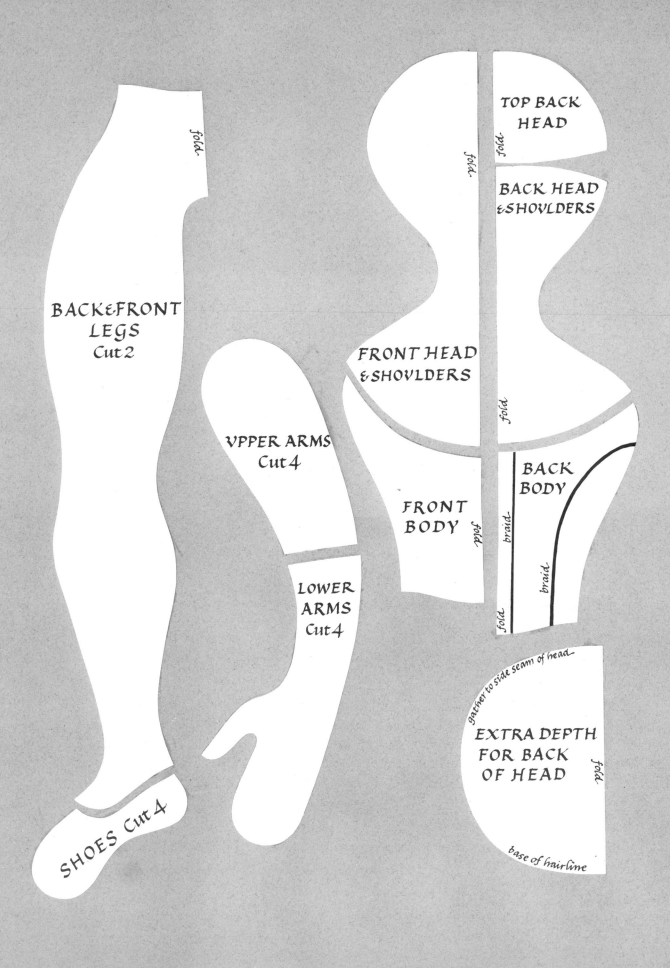

BASQVE SKIRT

fold centre back

STOMACHER

NOSE fold

gather

APRON

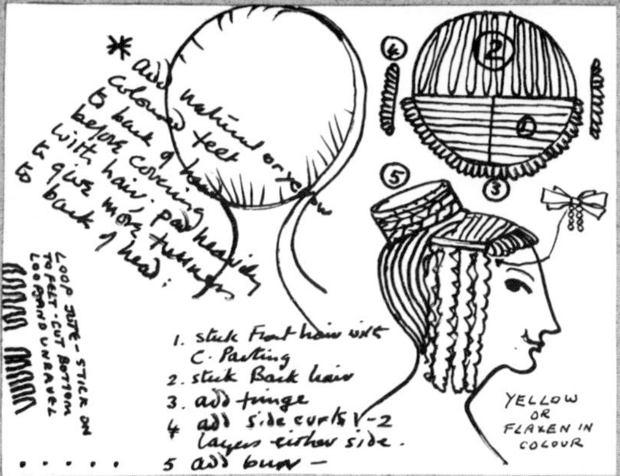
* add natural or yellow coloured felt to back of head before covering with hair; pad heavily to give more fullness to back of head;
LOOP JUTE - STICK ON TO FELT - CUT BOTTOM LOOPS AND UNRAVEL
1. stick Front hair with C. Parting
2. stick Back hair
3. add fringe
4 add side curls 1-2 layers either side.
5 add bun —
YELLOW OR FLAXEN IN COLOUR

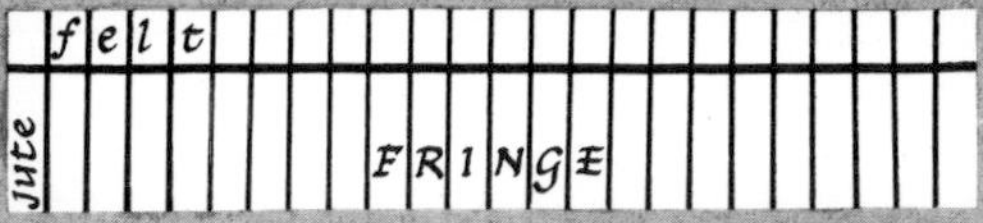
felt
jute
FRINGE

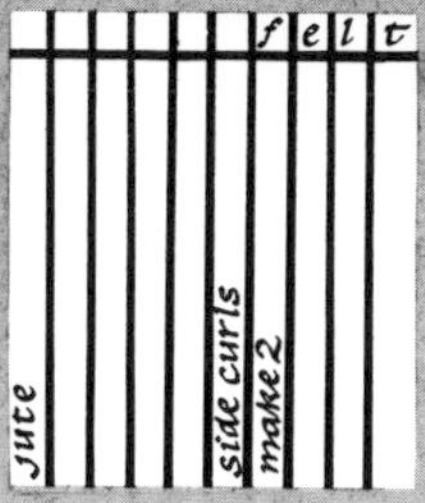
felt
jute
side curls
make 2

TOP of BUN FOUNDATION

SIDES to BUN FOUNDATION

gather

fold

PETTICOATS
1/4 scale

gather

fold

SKIRTS
1/4 scale

LE·CAPITAINE
Freely based on an engraving by Michel Lasne

56

LE CAPITAINE

Origins and Development

The caricature of a soldier can be traced back to the ancient Greek and Roman comedies. In the Italian Comedy he is a parody based on the soldiers of Italy, France and Spain. An adventurer and often a mercenary, the Captain develops into a satiric role based on the typical bombastic Spanish soldier – 'all honour and glory' – during the time of the Spanish wars. The soldier is also the basis for many other characters in the comedies, like the early Scaramouche, Polichinelle, Giangurgolo and perhaps Crispin. By the eighteenth century his popularity declines into a very minor role compared to his former glory. Don Armado in *Love's Labour's Lost* is Shakespeare's interpretation of this character.

Role

A figure of ridicule and always given highly descriptive names, in Italy had Spanish names like Sparento (terror), Terremoto (earthquake), Culonero (black arse), Sangre y Fuego (blood and fire), or Matamoros (killer of Moors). In France was given such names as Taille-Bras (wasp waist), Rodemont, or Fracasse (provoker of fights). Usually attended by a servant, his role was showy – flamboyant and vulgar in its vanity.

Character

A boasting, haughty, ambitious soldier; a braggart with an extravagant personality, and always over-ceremonious in his behaviour towards men as well as women. Pretentious and full of self-admiration, he claimed that he could not wear a shirt as the hairs on his chest so bristled with rage that the shirt would have been pierced full of holes! He also claimed he could eat only three kinds of meat: 'Jews, Lutherans and Turks', but on an isolated road at night he frightened himself almost to death.

The Mask

Early masks were flesh-coloured, with piercing eyes, menacing nose and fierce moustaches and pointed beard. By the seventeenth century the mask was usually discarded, and the actor painted his face to look pale in complexion with an arrogant expression. He still wore the sharply-pointed and fiercely turned-up moustaches, and an Imperial beard as pointed as the end of his sword. His hair was cut short or he wore the traditional black skullcap.

Costume

Followed the contemporary style of each period. Sometimes it was very colourful, even in bright yellows, and was always extremely elegant and well cut. Black, a favourite colour of Spain, was frequently chosen. By the eighteenth century he usually wore court costume of the time and of the country where he was performing. The character as interpreted in our figure is freely based on an early seventeenth-century engraving by Michel Lasne. He wears typical Spanish court costume: a peascod-bellied doublet with tabs forming the skirts, shoulder rolls or epaulettes, and well bombasted sleeves. The front of the doublet is fastened with rich gold buttons. The neckline and wrists terminate in large formally-set ruffs. The breeches are cut full at the waistline but narrow to fit at the knees. The cape, with collar, is semicircular and hangs to just below knee-level, made up in a rich red fabric which is unlike the rest of his costume, since his colour is entirely black, sombre but very rich in detail of braidings and buttoning in the Spanish style. His stockings are black and the shoes enriched with ties and buckles. The black silk high-crowned hat has a narrow brim and is decorated with a fine cockade of black and white feathers. As an alternative he could wear the narrow-brimmed black velvet beret which was fashionable during the second half of the sixteenth century. His sword can hang from his belt, but is often suspended from a richly decorated hanger.

Movement

The Captain struts around displaying and using his sword in a very flamboyant fashion, and with lots of extravagant bowing and flourishes absurdly overplayed, particularly when encountering a lady.

Speech, Voice and Other Skills

He has a nasal voice, speaking pompously in Spanish with a Castillian accent or a mixture of Spanish and Italian. The language is extravagant, declaiming at length on his conquests (usually mere fabrication) both on the battlefield and with women. The actor playing this role must be able to parody in an absurd and ridiculous manner the correct formalities and behaviour of a well-bred Spanish gentleman/soldier – including bows, gestures, sword-play, deportment etc.

Materials

Cotton: natural coloured (head, ears, nose, upper legs)
black velveteen (body, tabs, shoulder rolls, neck)
brushed black cotton (stockings, tab linings)
white (ruff foundations)

Silk: yellow patterned brocade (shoes and their tongues, tabs, body)
white (hands)
red (cape)
black-red (cape lining)
heavy white (ruffs)
red patterned (baldrick lining)
black watered silk (hat)

Fancy cloth (crepe): black with small gold spots (arms, shoulder rolls, breeches)

Lurex: black textured with gold (shoe, knee and belt rosettes; belt, kneebands)

Felt: black (skullcap, eyebrows, moustaches, beard)
red (mouth)
white (eyes)

Ribbon: black velvet (cape, body, arms, shoulder rolls) 8mm
black velvet embroidered with gold and spangles (sword hanger) *c.* 38mm

Braid: variety of various widths in gold (body, hat, arms, sword)
beige Russian (shoes)
brown Russian (skullcap)

Cord: gold (shoe ties)

Black ornamental buttons: (body)

Five large gold studs or buttons: (kneebands, shoes, belt)
Gold brooch or button: (hat)
Ornamental gold knob: (pommel to sword)
Black and white collection of feathers: (hat)
Black dye: (face features)
Thin gold metal or card: (hilt to sword)
Chopstick: (sword blade)
Card: (hat)
Drop pearl: (ear)
Padding

Making

Basic Figure: Join up all five sections which go to make the front body, sewing up the darts (X to X) on either side. Add a band of the yellow patterned brocade down the front, with black ornamental buttons set at regular intervals. Cover the side belly seams of the front body with gold braid, and edge the centre front band of brocade on either side with narrow black velvet ribbon. Assemble and sew all back and all front sections together. The front body waistline may need easing towards the centre front of the leg waistline to give the peascod belly fullness. (*Note:* the front and the back neck are made up in the black velveteen.) Sew completed front body to completed back body, turn right side out and pad.

Edge the top of the shoes with the beige Russian braid, adding the tongues, bows of gold cord, and rosettes of the Lurex centred with a gold button. Attach to the fronts. Cover the sides and base of the black skullcap with the brown Russian braid.

Assemble, make up and pad the arms, edging the seams all round as far as the wrists with gold braid. Do *not* attach them to the body.

Breeches: Make up according to patterns and gather and sew the waistline of the breeches to the waistline of the figure. Make sure that the side seams of the breeches correspond with the side seams of the body. Gather the bottom edges of the legs of the breeches to the join of stockings to upper legs. Cover these joins with a 12mm band of the Lurex, adding a rosette of the same material, centred with a gold button, to the outside seams of the legs.

Tabs: Line all the tabs with the black brushed cotton. Add three bands of the yellow patterned brocade to the front tab (see pattern) and sew it centrally to the front of the body waistline. Commencing from either side of the central tab, sew the remaining nine tabs around the rest of the waistline making sure that the fifth is placed centrally at the back. (Depending on the amount of padding placed in the figure they should overlap one another.)

Belt: The waistline is finished off with a belt of 20mm-wide Lurex, complete with a centrally placed rosette of the same material, and a gold button.

Arms and Shoulder Rolls: Now sew the arms firmly to the edge of the shoulders. Cover the shoulders with the shoulder rolls which are basically made up and sewn in position as described on p. 48 (l'Amant). Decorate the circumference of the rolls with 10mm-wide bands of the crepe, edged on either side with the narrow black velvet ribbon. Now sew the arms to the body.

Ruffs: Very long strips of the white silk will be required in making up the neck and cuff ruffs. Commence by sewing the top and bottom edges of the lengths of each ruff together, turn right side out, and press with the iron to make a good sharp edge at the fold line indicated on the patterns. Now fold each ruff up and down like a concertina to the depth of their foundations (lined with the same material). Next, taking each folded ruff, sew the *top* edges of the folds, *very closely packed together*, to the top edge of its foundation. Do the same with the bottom edge. Tightly place the ruffs around the throat (with the ends meeting at the centre back) and wrists of the figure, and firmly sew in position. Finish off by joining the ends of the ruff at the back of the head, and adding a band of black velvet ribbon around the lower part of the arms immediately above the top edges of the cuff ruffs.

Lastly catch each pleat to the next on the outside edges, alternately one third up and one third down, to form the figure of eight which is characteristic of the setting for this style of ruff. (See diagram accompanying the patterns.)

Hat: Make up as described on page 6, adding a gold braid hatband, and a cockade of black and white feathers positioned on the right-hand side. Finish off the base of the feathers with a rich brooch or buttons. Do *not* glue or sew the hat to the head.

Head: Make up the nose, pad with soft cottonwool, and sew in position. Then make up each ear in two thicknesses of the natural coloured cotton and interline with felt to stiffen them. Paint in the features with black, and then sew the ears to either side of the head, commencing on the same level as the top of the nose.

Now fix the hat squarely to the head.

Glue to the head all the felt features. First the black eyebrows, followed by the black moustache positioned immediately under the nose; then the red mouth with the black Imperial beard glued immediately beneath it, and lastly the white felt eyes.

Paint in with black the lines of the upper and lower eyelids, the pupils, the chin, and the little sneer on either side of the mouth. The face is now complete.

Sword Hanger: Line the embroidered black velvet ribbon with red patterned silk and join the two lower edges together. 12mm up from this edge back-stitch the back and front together to form a slot to hold the sword. Place on the figure across the chest and over the right shoulder.

Cape: Line the cape with the black/red silk. Then edge all round the red side with the black velvet ribbon set 12mm in. The collar of red is lined with the same material and is banded like the cape, around the sides and the top edge, with black velvet ribbon. Centre and oversew the collar to the top edge of the cape. Place on the figure, catching it on either shoulder at the commencement of the shoulder rolls to keep it in position.

Sword: Make up the hilt in thin gold metal or, which is easier, in two layers of gold card glued together. Then cut two holes in the hilt as marked on the pattern, and edge the perimeter of the hilt all round with gold braid to add enrichment. Place it on the chopstick 20mm down from the top, and, curving the hilt to take the hand, glue in position with epoxy glue. Using the same glue, stick the ornamental knob to the top of the chopstick, and the sword is complete to be placed in its hanger.

Accessories: Sew a drop pearl to the base of the left ear.

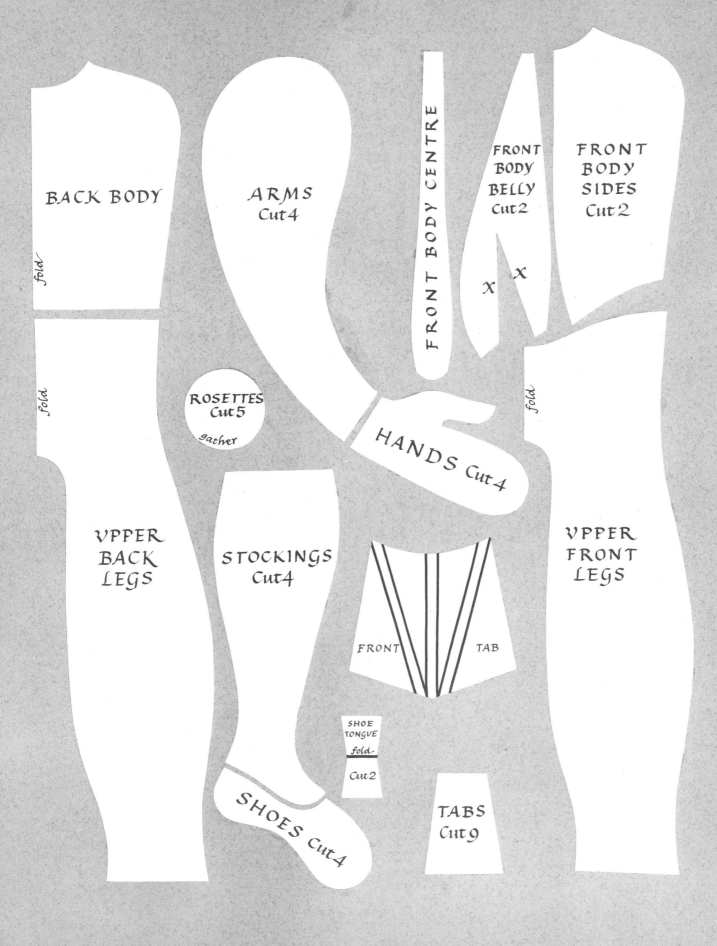

gather

gather

BREECHES FRONT

fold

gather

BREECHES BACK

gather

fold

SKVLLCAP BACK HEAD Cut 2

BACK HEAD Cut 2

BACK NECK

fold

FRONT HEAD

fold

FRONT NECK

fold

CAPE COLLAR ¼ scale

CAPE ¼ scale

EYEBROWS

Monstachs nearly sharp

NOSE

fold

fold centre back

BRIM TO HAT Cut 2

TOP of HAT

fold

BALDRICK

SHOVLDER ROLLS
Cut 4

BLACK FEATHERS

SPANISH CAPTAIN

BOMBASTED

SIDES of CROWN to HAT

fold lines

fold

fold lines

CVFF RUFFS
Cut 2

RVFF

fold

CVFF RVFFS foundation
Cut 2

RVFF foundation

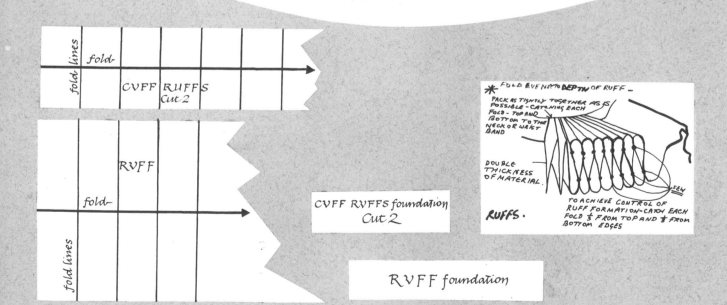

* FOLD EVENLY TO DEPTH OF RUFF —
PACK AS TIGHTLY TOGETHER AS IS
POSSIBLE — CATCHING EACH
FOLD — TOP AND
BOTTOM TO THE
NECK OR WAIST
BAND

DOUBLE
THICKNESS
OF MATERIAL

TO ACHIEVE CONTROL OF
RUFF FORMATION — CATCH EACH
FOLD ⅓ FROM TOP AND ⅓ FROM
BOTTOM EDGES

RUFFS.

GIANGURGOLO
Freely based on a print of the first half of the seventeenth century

62

GIANGURGOLO

Origins and Development

His home was Calabria and he seems to have gained little or no popularity with Parisian audiences. Giangurgolo is included in the collection of figures to show the wide range of the various military types who appeared in the comedies. Little information is available on this character.

Role

An overdressed, unsophisticated, loutish and stupid blockhead of a soldier. A clown and a figure of ridicule to be laughed at, Giangurgolo played a relatively minor role in the comedies.

Character

He pretends that he is a nobleman by birth, but is in reality very poor; conceited, and at times sad and melancholic. He scrounges and is a thief but has very little courage, even though he carries a long pointed sword, stealing out of necessity because of hunger; when he does obtain food he eats it ravenously. Lacking courage he easily gets frightened, and places himself in many awkward situations; authority scares him to death, and he only shows his temper and violence towards someone weaker than himself – usually a child or a cat. Though sensitive and nervous he was played as a 'show-off'.

The Mask

His mask was often just a long misformed phallic-shaped nose, which sometimes ended in a hairy wart, though he could have worn the half-mask terminating just below the cheeks.

Costume

The entire costume is predominantly striped in reds and yellows. He wears a buttoned-through doublet with full soft sleeves gathered in at the wrists, ending in softly-pleated turned-back cuffs – similar to the open, gathered, deep-falling double ruff at his throat. Over the doublet he wears a sleeveless coat or waistcoat which hangs free. His trousers terminate above the ankles and are tightish in fit. Over them, around the hips, he wears the once-fashionable (sixteenth century) bombasted 'slops'. The shoes are decorated and heeled. The great sword hangs at his left hip, carried by a wide hanger placed over the right shoulder and under the open waistcoat.

His hat is tall with a narrowish brim – untrimmed and very simple.

Movement

Ungainly, rough and peasant-like in his gaucheness, swaggering about in his colourful costume and carrying his great sword.

Speech, Voice and Other Skills

Conjectural: his speech was most likely coarse and vulgar and he probably spoke with a strong local dialect.

Materials

Cotton: natural coloured (head, ears, arms, body)
pink (legs)
grey (waistcoat lining, 'slops' foundation)

Silk: soft striped in reds, yellows and grey (doublet, sleeves, waistcoat, slops, and trousers)
brocade (hanger)
pink (hanger lining)
shot blue and lavender (shoes and their tongues)
Semi-transparent synthetic fabric: pink (neck frills and cuffs)
Braid: green (hat) 10mm
brocade (belt) 20mm
grey silk (waistcoat, trousers) 12mm
yellow Russian (shoes, mask)
gold (sword)
Silk upholstery fringe: ginger red (hair) 25mm
Ribbon: fancy mauve (shoes) 15mm
black velvet (wrists, neckline) 6mm
pink (doublet) 10mm
Felt: beige (hat)
yellow (mask)
white (face, eyes)
Simple decoration or button: (throat)
Pale blue mother-of-pearl buttons: (doublet)
Two ornamental buttons: (shoes)
Silver ornamental knob: pommel to sword)
Buckle: (belt)
Dye: pink (mouth)
black (face features)
Thin silver metal or card: (hilt to sword)
Chopstick: (sword blade)
Padding

Making

If striped material for the doublet, sleeves, waistcoat, slops and trousers is unobtainable, cut strips of pure silk 30mm wide, in red, yellow and lightly-patterned grey. Sew them together to make a length of cloth sufficient for all the patterns.

Basic Figure: Assemble and sew all front and all back sections together, easing or gathering the front body waistline to fit the front waistline of the legs. Sew completed front body to completed back body; turn right side out and pad.

The lower edge of the yellow felt mask is then covered with two bands of the yellow Russian braid. Edge the top of the shoes also with the yellow Russian braid, adding to the fronts the tongues (made up in the same material as the shoes – the fold joining the shoes) and fancy mauve ribbon bows each centred with an ornamental button.

Assemble, make up and pad the arms. Then making up the striped sleeves, place on the arms and sew and gather the lower edges to the wrist lines, and the heads to the tops of the arms – simulating the line of an armhole. Finish off the wrist lines with upstanding gathered cuffs of the semi-transparent pink material, covering the joins with narrow bands of black velvet ribbon. The arms are now finished but do *not* attach them to the body.

Doublet: The doublet is cut from the same patterns that go to make up the body. Add a band of the pink ribbon, with the small pale blue mother-of-pearl buttons set at regular intervals, down the centre front of the body. Now sew the back and front together, leaving the shoulder seams sufficiently open at the neck edge for placing the doublet onto the body. When this has been done, finish sewing up the shoulder seams and sew the neckline to the figure.

Lastly, sew the waistline edge to the body, easing or gathering the front so that the side seams of the doublet correspond with the side seams of the body.

Trousers: Make up according to pattern, edging the ends of the legs with the grey silk braid. Place on the figure and gather the waistline evenly to the waistline edge of the doublet. Sew in position.

Slops: Make up the foundation to the slops in the grey cotton. Then make up the slops proper. Gather the top edge of the slops evenly to the top edge of the foundation, repeating the same process at the lower edge. Now place the waistline of the finished slops to the waistline on the figure where the trousers meet the doublet. Sew in position.

Belt: The waistline is finished off with a 20mm belt of patterned braid, complete with buckle.

Neckline: Trim with two gathered tiers of the semi-transparent pink material, leaving it open in front. Cover the neckline edge with a band of the black velvet ribbon, adding a simple button placed at the centre front of the throat. Now sew the arms firmly to the edges of the shoulders.

Waistcoat: Line the fronts and the back with the grey cotton. Oversew the fronts to the back and band all round the edges of the waistcoat with the grey silk braid. Now place it on the figure.

Hat: Make up the brim in two thicknesses of beige felt, glueing them together. Then make up the crown, place it over a small circular bowl or a wooden ball; freely apply water to a cloth to cover the hat and, with a very hot iron, shrink and stretch the felt to follow the curve of the bowl or ball.

Check the size of the inner circumference of the brim and crown, to fit the size of the head, and then, trimming the lower edge of the crown (it will have become uneven due to the shrinking and stretching process), oversew it to the inner circumference of the brim. Decorate the join of crown to brim with a simple band of dull green braid. At the back of the hat glue to the inside of the crown a 15cm strip of ginger silk upholstery fringe, simulating the hair. Do not fix the hat to the head until the ears have been sewn in position.

Head and Mask: First make up each ear in two thicknesses of the natural coloured cotton, interlined with felt to stiffen them. Paint in the features, and sew the completed ears to the sides of the head, beginning at the base of the mask.

The hat can now be sewn or glued well to the back of the head.

Glue the white muzzle immediately below the edge of the mask, then the white felt eyes. The smiling mouth is painted in pink, but all the other features are drawn in with black, including the eyes and eyebrows, the top edge of the mouth, and the cheeks.

Sword Hanger: Make up in some richly-patterned brocade, lining it with pink silk. Join the angled ends together and decorate with braid. Lastly back-stitch together the front and back of the hanger 20mm up from the base to form a slot to hold the sword. Now place it on the figure, across the chest and over the right shoulder underneath the waistcoat.

Sword: Assemble and make as described on p. 58 (le Capitaine). The hilt should be richly decorated around its edge with gold braid. When completed place the sword in its hanger.

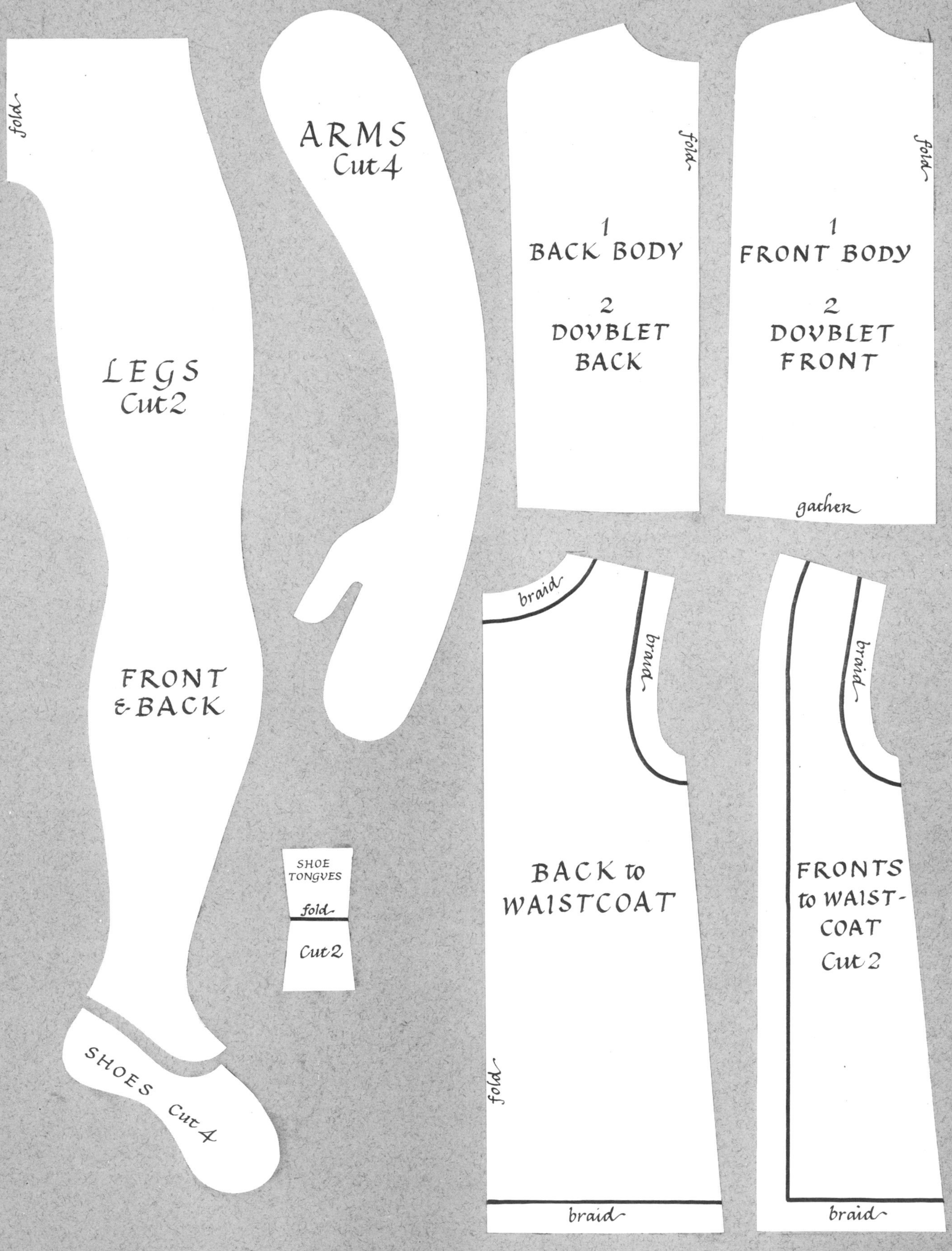

ARMS
Cut 4

LEGS
Cut 2

FRONT
& BACK

fold

SHOE
TONGVES
fold
Cut 2

SHOES   Cut 4

1
BACK BODY

2
DOVBLET
BACK

fold

1
FRONT BODY

2
DOVBLET
FRONT

fold

gather

braid

braid

BACK to
WAISTCOAT

fold

braid

braid

braid

FRONTS
to WAIST-
COAT
Cut 2

braid

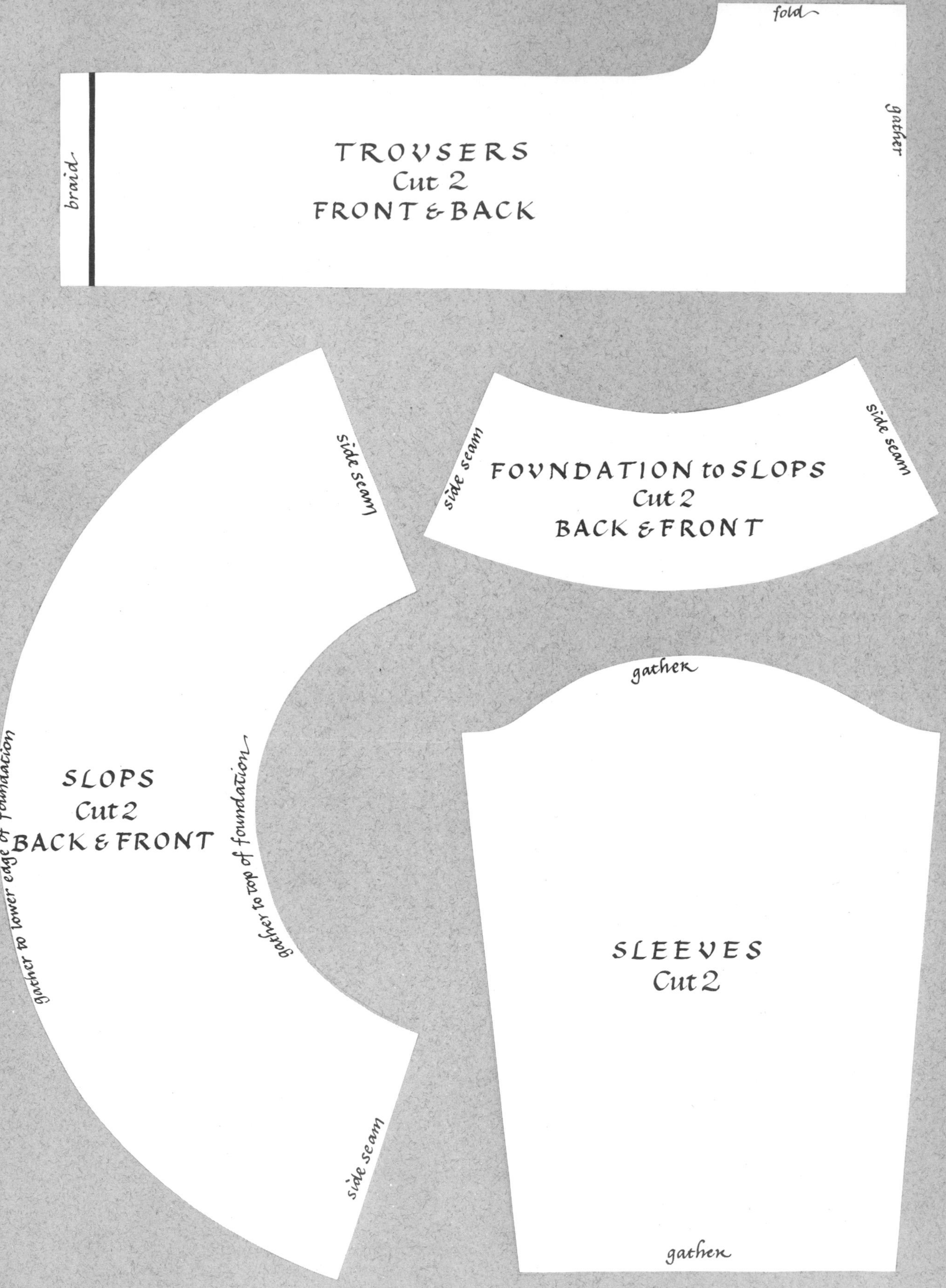

TROVSERS
Cut 2
FRONT & BACK

fold

gather

braid

side seam

side seam

FOVNDATION to SLOPS
Cut 2
BACK & FRONT

side seam

gather

SLOPS
Cut 2
BACK & FRONT

gather to lower edge of foundation

gather to top of foundation

SLEEVES
Cut 2

side seam

gather

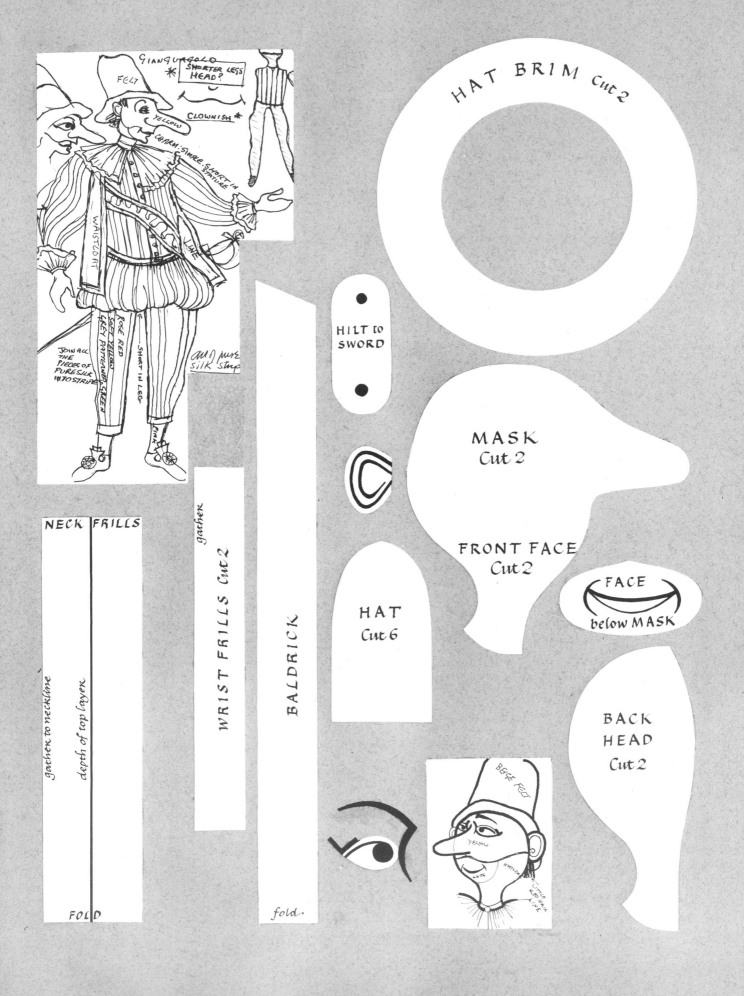

GIANGURGOLO
FELT
SHORTER LESS HEAD?
CLOWNISH *
YELLOW
CHARM: SIMPLE SHORT IN STATURE
WAISTCOAT
LINE
ROSE RED
SOFT YELLOW
GREY PATTERNED GREEN
JOIN ALL THE PIECES OF PURE SILK INTO STRIPES
SHIRT IN LEG
AND MORE SILK STRIPES
PINK

HAT BRIM Cut 2

HILT to SWORD

MASK Cut 2

FRONT FACE Cut 2

FACE below MASK

NECK FRILLS

gather

WRIST FRILLS Cut 2

BALDRICK

HAT Cut 6

BACK HEAD Cut 2

gather to neckline

depth of top layer

FOLD

fold

BEIGE FELT
YELLOW
WHITE
LITTLE OR NO HAIR
LITTLE GREY HAIR LINE

SCARAMOUCHE
Based on an engraving by Nicholas Bonnart of Tiberio Fiorilli

SCARAMOUCHE

Origins and Development

Called Scaramuccia and coming from Naples in Italy sometime during the early part of the sixteenth century, the role was originally that of a Captain, dressed completely in black, who loved fighting with his long pointed sword and had the agility and speed of a mosquito. This interpretation was completely changed by the great Tiberio Fiorilli (1604?-1696?). He too came from Naples, and was an outstanding favourite at the court of Louis XIV and enormously admired by Molière ('He was Molière's master, his own was nature' runs the caption underneath one of Fiorilli's portraits). The role and interpretation became Fiorilli's own until his death, after which the character began to disappear from the comedies.

Role

As created by Fiorilli, Scaramouche was valet to an impecunious gentleman. He was often in confederacy with Pulcinella, even though their characters were very different. Most of the time they quarrel amongst themselves, and then, becoming friends, enjoy frightening bystanders with their behaviour and sometimes just muddle up the story-line of the scenario.

Character

He loves complicated intrigues and his character is full of laughter, cunning, and at times sadness. Slippery as a fish, he enjoys talking about the great wealth and noble birth of the gentleman he serves, who in reality is very poor. Scaramouche always liked drinking and women. He picked pockets, stole when he could from his impoverished master, but somehow always managed to make an escape when faced with trouble. Molière based his character Sganarelle on Fiorilli's Scaramouche in *le Cocu magnifique*. This is only one of the many plays where Molière adapted and used this particular characterisation.

The Mask

Originally the role was played with a mask, but Fiorilli discarded it, simply powdering his face white and accentuating the black arched eyebrows, the drooping 'Viva Zapata' moustaches, and the little pointed Imperial beard.

Costume

Entirely in black, but with touches of white in the form of a frilled collar and cuffs ('the sky this evening is dressed like Scaramouche' wrote Molière), he wears a skirted buttoned-through jacket with tightly-fitting sleeves terminating at the shoulders with epaulettes. The jacket is held in at the waist by a sash or belt, and he sometimes carries a purse. The breeches are full and gathered in at the knees, finishing in simple ties. The soft shoes, like his stockings, are also black. He wears an enormous black mantle or cloak which he drapes about himself, sometimes allowing it to trail on the ground, though there is a print showing Scaramouche dancing and wearing the short buttock-length cape which was fashionable during the latter part of the sixteenth century. The hat is a large floppy beret falling down at the back, at times below shoulder level. Fiorilli carried the sword, and he also carred a beribboned mandolin or guitar to accompany himself when singing.

Movement

Fiorilli's great gift was the art of mime and dancing – often at times speaking very little. His skill was based on mimetic improvisations, and it is recorded that he could keep his audience laughing for over a quarter of an hour merely by showing fear and panic without uttering a single word.

Speech, Voice and Other Skills

When he does speak, his imagination can concoct the most outlandish and flamboyant stories of his various escapades and adventures. Scaramouche dances, plays many musical instruments, sings, conjures and can introduce into his performance the skill of the stage magician.

Fiorilli was very agile, and even when he was over eighty he could still kick himself or an opponent in the face.

Materials

Cotton: white (face, nose, upper legs)
  natural coloured (hands)
  glazed grey-green (guitar)
  soft white (cuffs)
  dull brown (skirt lining)
Crepe: black (mantle, beret, breeches)
Silk velvet: black (mantle)
Cotton velveteen: black (body, arms, skirts)
Shot silk: black-purple (stockings)
Silk: black (shoes, epaulette linings)
Patterned brocade: (guitar)
Lurex: gold and black striped (guitar)
Satin: black (beret, sash)
Broderie anglaise: white (neck frill) 35mm
Ribbon: black (arms, breeches, guitar) 12mm
  black velvet (epaulettes, shoes) 10mm
  white (guitar) 12mm
  dull brown (body) 12mm
Braid: black Russian (shoes)
Gold ornamental button: (sash)
Four black cloth-covered buttons: (shoes, kneebands)
Black ornamental buttons: (body)
Felt: black (guitar, epaulettes, eyebrows, beard, moustaches, neckline)
  red (mouth)
  grey (eyes, face features)
Dye: black (face features)
Semicircular dowel rod: (guitar)
Card: (guitar)
Padding

Making

Basic Figure: Add a band of dull brown ribbon down the centre front of the body, with the small black ornamental buttons set at regular intervals. Assemble and sew all front and all back sections together; then sew the completed front body to completed back body, turn right side out and pad. Edge the top of the shoes with the black Russian braid, adding small black velvet ribbon bows, centred with a black cloth-covered button, to the fronts.

Assemble, make up and pad the arms, covering the seams all round, as far as the wrists, with black ribbon, adding 25mm deep frills of white gathered cotton to the wrists. Cover the join of frills to wrists with a band of the black ribbon. The arms are now complete, but do *not* attach them to the body.

Breeches: Make up the breeches in black crepe and put them on the figure, gathering and sewing the waist edge to the waistline of the body and the ends of the legs to the join of stockings to the upper legs. Cover the joins with a banding of the black ribbon, forming the kneebands, and finish off on the outside seam of each leg with a black cloth-covered button.

Skirts: Line with the dull brown cotton, then gather and sew the waistline to the waistline of the body. This join is covered by the sash.

Sash: Hem the sash of black satin and reduce its depth with soft horizontal pleats. Now place it around the waistline of the figure and sew it in position, joining the two ends 25mm forward from the left-hand side seam of the body. Make up the two rosettes in the same material, centring the smaller rosette to the centre of the larger rosette; decorate the double rosette with a gold ornamental button sewn to its centre. Now sew the finished rosette to the sash to cover the join of the sash on the left-hand side.

Arms and Epaulettes: Sew the arms firmly to the edge of the shoulders. Cover the shoulders with epaulettes of black felt (lined with black silk) banded all round with the black velvet ribbon.

Neck Frill: Trim the neckline with a gathered frill of white *broderie anglaise*, terminating at the neckline edge with a 6mm band of black felt.

Hat: Make up the rim of the beret in black satin, stiffening the back with felt. Gather the top of the beret (made up in the black crepe) evenly to the top edge of the rim.

Now leave the hat until the head is complete save for the eyes and painted features.

Head: Make up the nose, pad it with soft cottonwool, and sew in position. Glue to the face the eyebrows, moustache and beard in black felt; glue also to the head the red felt mouth and the grey felt continuation of the smile on either side of the moustaches.

Now return to the beret. Softly pad the beret to control its shape and to add extra bulk to the back of the head, and sew or glue in position. Depending on the amount of padding placed in the head, the rim of the beret may need to be eased to fit.

Cut the eyes from grey felt, and angle them to the face so that they have the right cunning and melancholy expression before glueing them. Lastly paint in black the upper eyelids, the eyes, and the smile.

Shoulder Mantles: There are two mantles: one made up in the black silk velvet and the other in the black crepe. Hem the edges of the black velvet rectangle, gathering one end to the width of the shoulder. Then sew the gathered end to the left shoulder seam of the figure. This mantle hangs down the back and is looped up and caught in position, with light stitching, to the top of the right epaulette, with the remaining length of the mantle falling down the side of the figure.

The second mantle, of black crepe hemmed all round, is gathered and sewn to the width of the same shoulder, allowing about a third of the length of the material to fall down the front of the body and the remaining longer length to fall down the back.

Accessories: The guitar is made up and carried exactly the same way as Brighella's (see page 22). The top and lower surfaces of the instrument are covered in patterned brocade to simulate marquetry and the sides are of glazed grey-green cotton. The fingerboard of semicircular dowel rod is covered with the striped Lurex and the guitar face is finished off with an oval of black felt. The flowing streamers of ribbon are in black and white.

fold

ARMS
Cut 4

FRONT BODY

BACK BODY

BACK & FRONT
VPPER LEGS

Cut 2

fold

fold

HANDS
Cut 2

gather

c. back fold

BACK SKIRTS

semi-circular dowel rod

sides to guitar

STOCKINGS
Cut 4

gather

side seam

FRONT SKIRTS
Cut 2

SHOES Cut 4

GVITAR
Cut 2

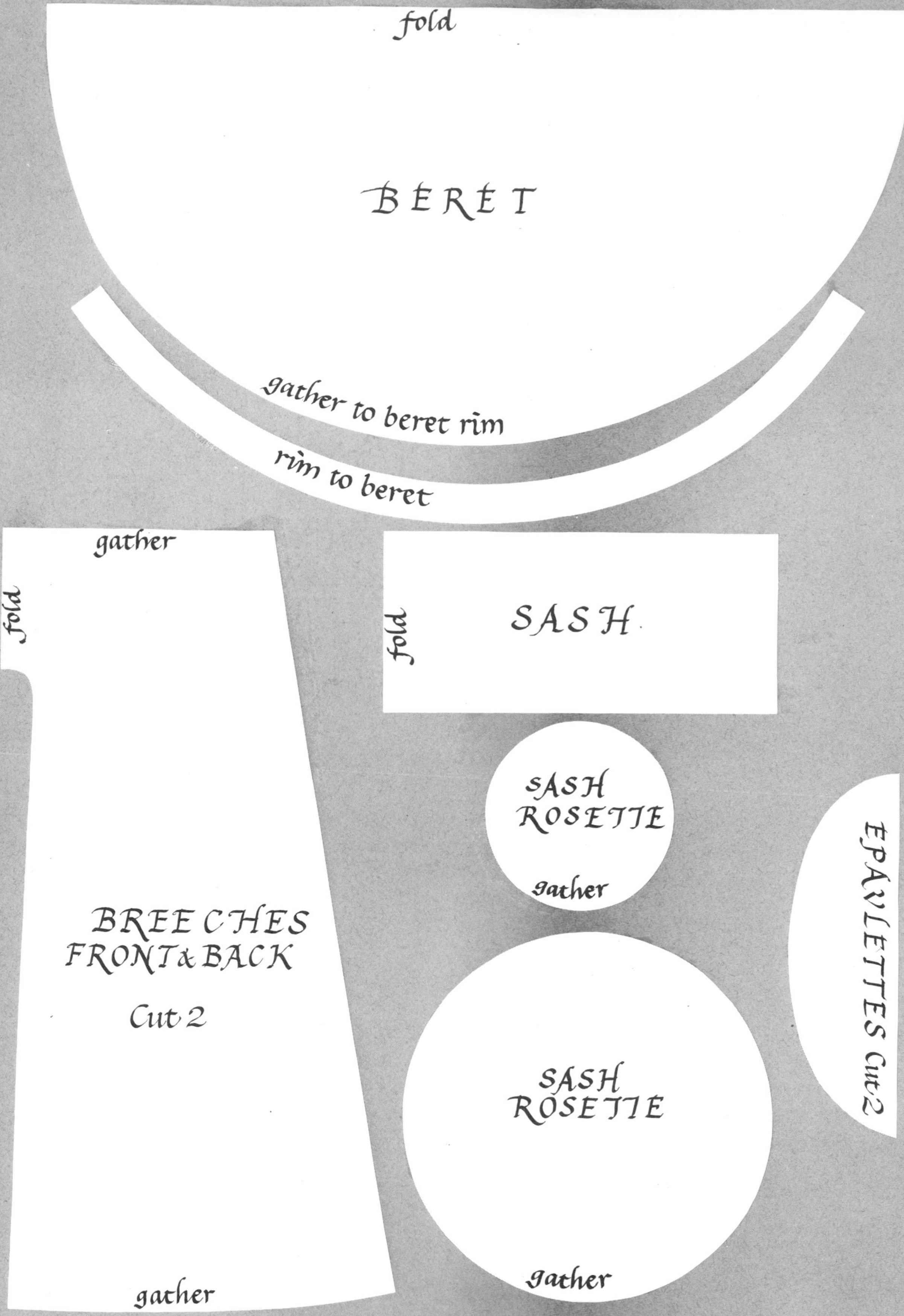

fold

BERET

gather to beret rim

rim to beret

gather

fold

fold

SASH

SASH
ROSETTE

gather

EPAULETTES Cut 2

BREECHES
FRONT & BACK

Cut 2

SASH
ROSETTE

gather

gather

gather

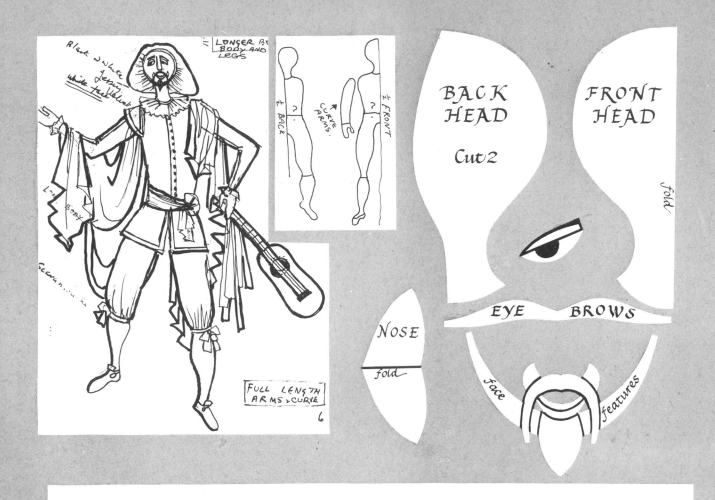

LONGER B
BODY AND
LEGS

Black & White
& white
White Feather

Long Body

FULL LENGTH
ARMS CURVE

6

½ BACK

CURVE
ARMS.

½ FRONT

BACK
HEAD

Cut 2

FRONT
HEAD

fold

EYE   BROWS

NOSE

fold

face   features

SWAG for SHOVLDER MANTLE
¼ scale

SWAG for SHOVLDER MANTLE
¼ scale

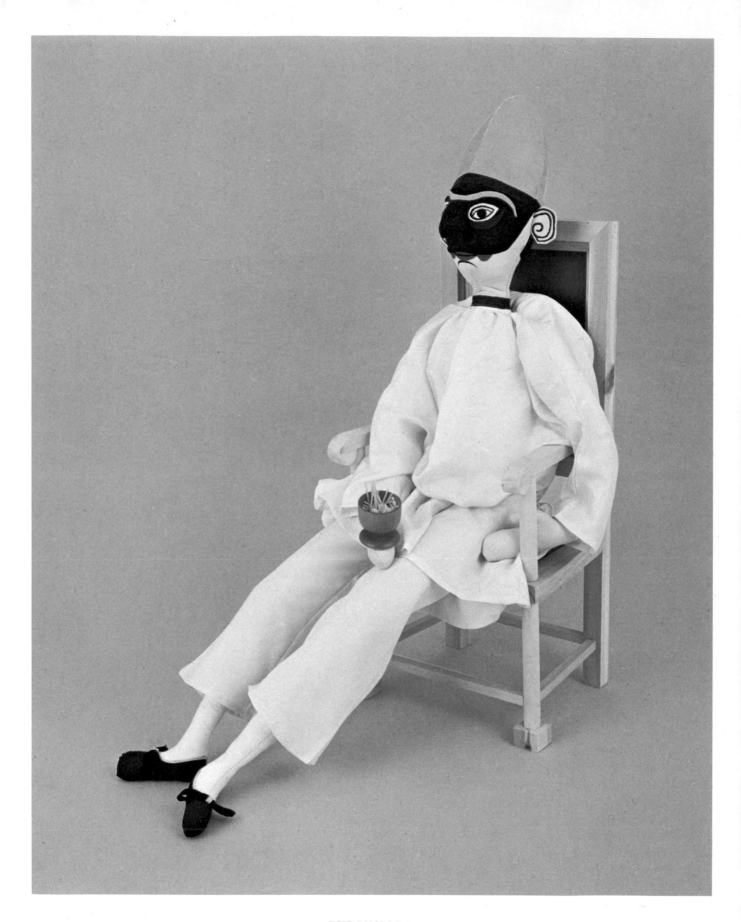

PULCINELLA
Based on the traditional white costume

74

PVLCINELLA

Origins and Development

Pulcinella's origin lies in obscurity though he has much in common with the 'grotesques' who appeared in the old Greek and Roman comedies. In the Commedia he originally came from Acerra in Campania, but found his natural home in Naples. Sometimes he was called Citrulo (= stupid), then Pulcino (= a small chicken) from which he derived his eventual name. There were various interpretations in the playing of this role. We know he existed in the sixteenth century and that he spawned many similar characters. Usually Pulcinella was, or could be, very grotesque, with overhanging belly and a humpback – sometimes he appeared with two humps (dual-personality). Duchartre refers to Pulcinella as the 'father' of Polichenelle who in turn became England's Mr Punch.

Pulcinella was a particularly popular character, and we see him appearing in most of the capitals of Europe, especially at markets, in puppet booths, at fairs and carnivals right through into the nineteenth century, often performing as a solo act. Sometimes whole groups of Pulcinellas are seen appearing together, as for example in the drawings of Domenico Tiepolo, usually in a roofed booth-type theatre, engaged in tumbling acrobatics, and performing on the slackwire or trapeze. Michangelo Francanzani, from Naples, who played this role, appeared in Paris in 1665 and was a great success at the court of Louis XIV, being paid handsomely for his performances. It is said that he played without a mask.

Role

He could be a servant, a person from the countryside, physician or soldier, or would take on any job coming his way. He liked a good fight and was frequently very cruel. He lived an isolated and lonely life; not trusting the world he is rarely seen with a lover, close friend, wife or family. Pulcinella is an enigmatic character – he can be cruel, vain, kind, timorous, funny or frightening, and cannot be trusted. His dual personality is difficult to define, but with his deformities it is possible to understand both the cruel and vicious side of his nature and his moments of kindness. Pulcinella can be played young or old, but usually he is middle-aged and obese.

Character

Typically Neapolitan by nature, he was originally very coarse and brutal but mellowed somewhat with time. His character is as complex as that of Arlequin, but he does not possess Arlequin's gaiety. He cannot keep a secret and is often a coward feigning simpleness, playing the idiot with abandonment. He is very shrewd and capable of getting himself out of most of the problems he creates for himself – even at the expense of a good beating. It is said that he will give his food, usually pasta already in his mouth, to someone hungrier than himself. Amusingly, he eats his food with ravenous appetite, from a horn-shaped container like a shell, a pot, or even a chamber-pot!

The Mask

Originally it was a full mask with long moustaches and pointed beard, but by the seventeenth century it usually covered only the upper part of the face and he no longer wore the beard and moustache. The colour was black or dark in tone and the nose was long and beaked like a bird. To add to his deformities he had a large protuberance or carbuncle on his cheek or forehead; his expression was cold and cruel with sharp eyes. The hair was concealed by the traditional black skullcap.

Costume

Is of ancient peasant origin – just a simple very loose white tunic, tied in at the waist, and fullish trousers. Over his skullcap he wore a tall sugarloaf-shaped hat of grey, white or some other simple neutral colour. He often carried a wooden sword (echoes of Arlequin) and a purse fastened to his girdle. In France during the seventeenth century some actors playing this role adopted the costume worn by the French Polichinelle, but in the eighteenth century, when they returned to Italy, they reverted to the original costume.

Movement

Very fast and agile, and mostly on the move in a hopping, skipping walk or half run; but he could equally be very slow and lazy in his behaviour. He constantly uses his arms and hands with broad gestures, and it is difficult for him to remain still.

Speech, Voice and Other Skills

A clucking, squeaking voice when speaking, and never knowing when to stop. The actor playing this role had to be an excellent acrobat, performing frequently on the trapeze or slackwire; he also danced, sang, and was skilled in the art of mimicry and mime – impersonating birds, animals, trees and even houses. We are reminded of Pulcinella's dual personality when he pretends he does not know that he is on stage and in front of an audience, and behaves as if he were in his own home or in a street, defecating or urinating until another actor reminds him where he is – in public and in a play. Then he immediately returns to playing the situation as outlined in the scenario.

Materials

Cotton: natural coloured (face, arms, ears)
    white (hump, body and legs)
    grey twill (hat)
    indigo blue (shoes)
Soft silk: white (tunic, trousers)
Felt: brown (mask, skullcap)
    lighter brown (mask features)
    black (mask features)
    grey (eyebrows)
    red (mouth and face features)
    white (eyes)
Braid: yellow Russian (shoes)
    black Russian (mask, skullcap)
Ribbon: black (shoes) 12mm
    indigo blue (neckline, hat) 12mm
Dye: black (face features)
Brown felt-covered button: (carbuncle)
Goblet: for macaroni or pasta
Padding

Making

Basic Figure: *Omit* from the pattern the mouth and the red cheeks when making up the basic figure (see pattern of mask), and cut the front and back body from the same pattern. Assemble and sew all front and all back sections together; then sew the completed front body to completed back body, turn right side out and pad. Now sew the hump to the back, padding it firmly with cottonwool, gathering the lower edge (X to X) following the pattern, and the neck edge to fit the neckline.

Band all round the lower edge of the mask and the skullcap with the black Russian braid. Edge the top of the shoes with the yellow Russian braid, adding small bows of black ribbon bound in the centres with the yellow Russian braid, to the fronts.

Assemble, make up and pad the arms, but do *not* attach them to the edge of the shoulders until the trousers have been finished.

Trousers: Make up in the soft white silk, hemming the bottoms of the legs. Place the trousers on the figure, gathering the waist edge evenly to the waistline of the body, and sew in position.

Arms: Now sew the arms firmly to the edge of the shoulders.

Tunic: Make up the tunic, hemming the skirts, the ends of the sleeves, and the neckline, *but* leave the shoulder seams unsewn from the neckline edge as far as is necessary to put the tunic onto the figure. Place a line of gathering (do not gather yet) to the line as indicated on the patterns.

Now place the tunic onto the figure, sewing up the unsewn shoulder seams; gather and sew the neckline around the base of the neck. Finish off the neck edge with a band of the indigo blue cotton ribbon.

Lastly draw up the gathering thread around the tunic to the *natural* waistline measurement of the figure, making sure that the side seams of the tunic correspond to the side seams of the body. When sewn to the body the finished result should produce a pouched effect at the waist.

Hat: The hat of grey twill is in four sections sewn together – centre front to centre front, centre back to centre back, and side seams to side seams. Place and sew the hat high on the head. When sewn, cover the edge with a band of the indigo blue cotton ribbon. (It is helpful to pad the inside of the hat lightly to keep it permanently upright.)

Head and Mask: Make up each ear in two thicknesses of the natural coloured cotton with an interlining of felt to stiffen them. Paint in the features and then sew the completed ears to either side of the head

Glue the grey felt eyebrows high on the forehead, then the mouth and red cheeks to the edge of the bottom of the mask (see pattern). From a scrap of black felt cut a 'frown', and glue it above the centre of the eyebrows. Next place the white felt eyes to the head with the light brown felt features immediately beneath them, and glue all four pieces in position. The features – eyes, smile and chin – are all painted in black dye or poster colour. Complete by adding a brown felt-covered button (simulating a carbuncle) high on the right cheek.

Accessories: Glue a goblet of your own invention, full of macaroni, in his hand. It could be shaped like a chamber pot. The goblet in the sculpture was a wooden egg-cup painted orange, with the pasta glued to the inside.

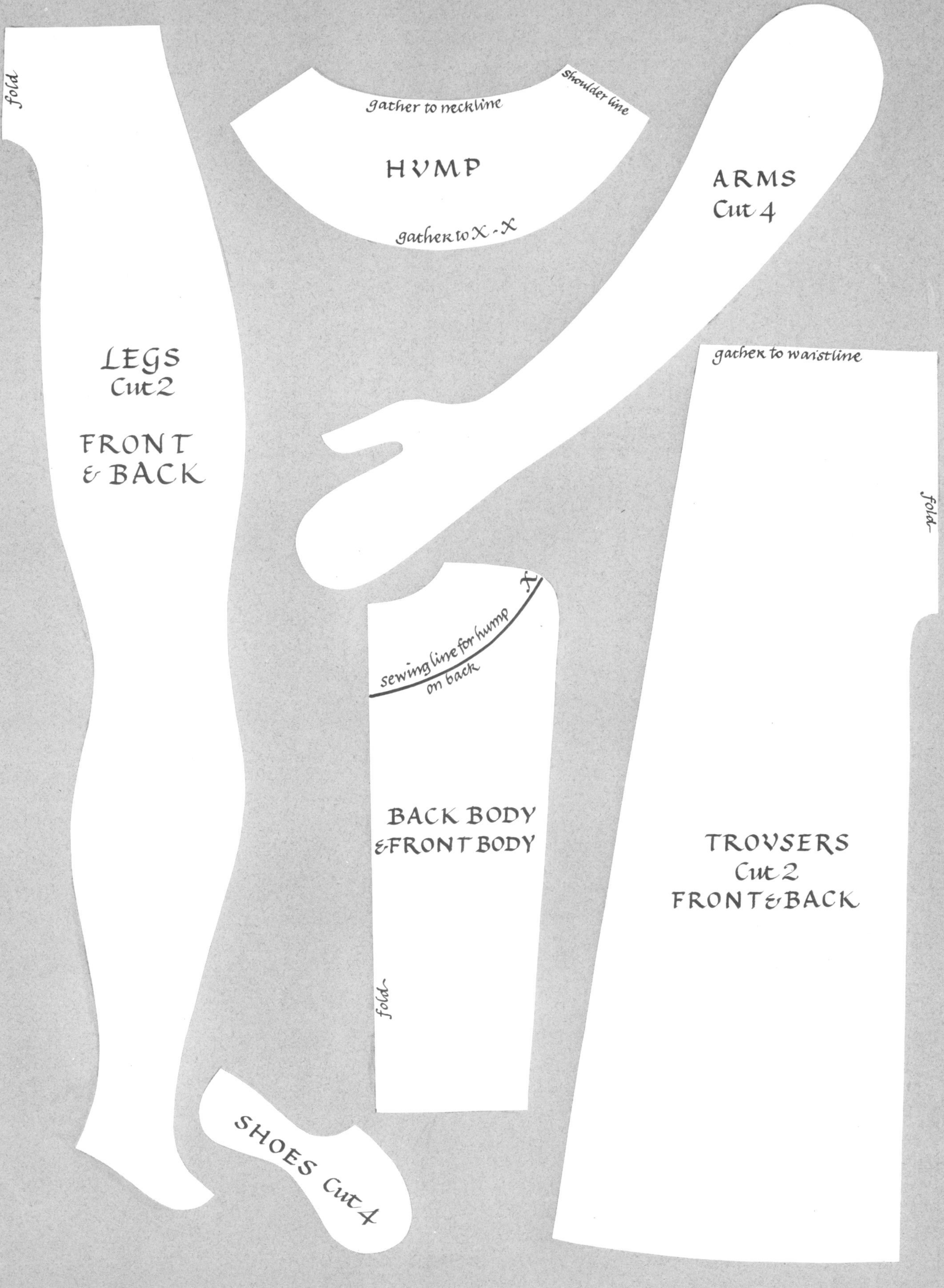

fold

LEGS
Cut 2

FRONT
& BACK

gather to neckline

shoulder line

HVMP

gather to X - X

ARMS
Cut 4

gather to waistline

fold

X

sewing line for hump
on back

BACK BODY
& FRONT BODY

fold

TROVSERS
Cut 2
FRONT & BACK

SHOES Cut 4

TVNIC FRONT

fold

MASK FRONT
Cut 2

FACE FRONT
Cut 2

gathering line

BACK of HEAD
(SKVLLCAP)
Cut 2

BACK
NECK
Cut
2

TVNIC BACK

fold

gathering line

HAT BACK
Cut 2

CB

HAT FRONT
Cut 2

CF

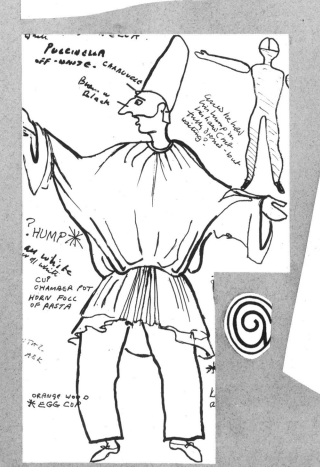

PUCCINELLA
off-white. CARAUUGE

Brown u
Black

? HUMP *

an white
all white

CUP
CHAMBER POT
HORN FOLL
OF PASTA

ORANGE WOOD
* EGG CUP

POLICHINELLE

Based on the engraving after a lost painting by Watteau

80

POLICHINELLE

Origins and Development

Polichinelle is a French invention and has distinct connections with the Italian Pulcinella, though it would be wrong to link him with Pulcinella other than by the similarities in their deformities, their acts of cruelty and their squeaking voice. Both existed in their own right. Polichinelle could have developed from the French deformed court jester and, further back in time, from the 'grotesques' popular in the old Greek and Roman plays. Some authorities suggest that he was a bizarre parody based on the French or Gascon captain. The only French source for him so far found is in an engraving after a lost painting by Watteau showing the eviction of the Italian players from Paris by order of Louis XIV in 1697; there he is a strutting, flamboyantly-dressed military character.

He seems to have played a relatively minor role in the comedies, but as England's Mr Punch, recorded as far back as the 1650s, he became a universal figure and the most celebrated of all glove puppets in the Punch and Judy shows, which included characters like his wife, their baby, death, the devil, a hangman, and later a policeman and a crocodile. His costume as a puppet, though still retaining all the deformities, is closer in style to the dress worn by a medieval or Elizabethan court jester than that of a soldier.

Role

A very malicious and vicious military man – the most deformed of all the characters in the Commedia. As a puppet (and this must give some indication to his character in France) he beats his wife, throws his baby around, defies death, the devil and the hangman, and is completely fearless. To keep up this image, he constantly hits out with a wooden club and shouts in a high-pitched, squeaking voice.

Character

Small in stature, and a 'show off', he brags in the most macabre terms about the number of people he has killed, referring to 'the bones and skulls of soldiers, sergeants, and the tongues of women' with which he paved the streets of Paris! Though blood-thirsty and menacing he was treated as a figure of fun to be laughed at by his audiences.

The Mask

There seems to be no evidence that the character wore a mask in France, but in the obscure past he must have done so to accentuate the large phallic-shaped nose and jutting chin. Probably the French actors in the seventeenth century resorted to building out their own nose and chin with a form of putty, painting their features in with a vicious, conceited and defiant expression, and playing the role with a wicked glint in their eyes.

Costume

By the middle of the seventeenth century the costume was a preposterous parody of the court costume fashionable at the end of the late sixteenth century. The heavily padded, huge, peascod-bellied doublet had short skirts; epaulettes or shoulder rolls had short puffed-out sleeves covering the upper parts of the arms, with the sleeves proper bombasted and terminating at the wrists. The breeches were tight, knee-length and decorated at the sides with flamboyant rosettes like the shoes. A large ruff '*à la confusion*' was worn at the neck, and the wrist ruffles were either made up in the same fashion or just gathered. He always appeared with a large humped back, sometimes two humps, and the bright and gaudy colours (and the profusion of rich braidings covering his entire costume) perhaps made up for his distorted body.

It is equally possible that the multi-coloured costume he wore was a reminder of the colours worn by the jesters, fools and deformed buffoons of earlier times. All the colours were bright as a circus or fairground – reds, yellows, blues, oranges, sometimes greens, and gold. He wore (French fashion) a tall black brimmed hat set off with a large cockade of multicoloured feathers.

Movement

He strutted around like a cock, sticking out his great belly in a caricature of military fashion. His walk was akin to the 'goose-step', but Polichinelle was, at the same time, very agile and speedy when necessity called for making a quick get-away.

Speech, Voice and Other Skills

He had a clucking, high-pitched voice which sometimes resembled the crowing of a cock. He may have appeared clumsy but he used his club like a good swordsman.

Materials

Imagination can be used in the choice of bright and gaudy colours for his costume. Select as many different textures and gold braids as possible. The braiding cannot be overdone.

Cotton: white (head, ears, hands, foundation for ruff)
    pink (stockings)
    multi-coloured patterned (rosettes for shoes, kneebands and belt)
    brightly patterned yellow and red (body and hump)
    patterned deep blue (body, skirts, arms, upper legs)
    orange (skirts, arms, upper legs, sides to hump)
    bright red (binding of epaulettes, skirt lining)
Silk: orange (puff sleeves)
    black (hat)
    brown (shoes)
    rose-red (epaulettes)
Ribbon: black velvet (body) 12mm
    red silk (wrists, upper legs, body) 10mm
    narrow red (hat)
    embroidered or fancy (puff sleeves, kneebands, belt) 24mm
Lace: broad gold (ruff and wrist frills) 35mm
Braid: gold (hat) 10mm
    various types of gold braid (body, skirts, arms, upper legs)
    brown Russian (shoes)
    black Russian (to hang club from wrist)

Felt: beige (face)
　　　 pink (face)
　　　 red (eyes)
Gold buttons: body)
Brooch or buckle: (belt)
Rich brooch or ornament: (hat)
Variety of multi-coloured feathers: (hat)
Dye: black (face features)
Card: (hat)
Wooden club
Padding

Making

Basic Figure: Join up the six sections which go to make up the front body: the two centre pieces in yellow and red patterned cotton, the next two sections in the deep blue patterned cotton, and the outer two sections in the yellow and red patterned cotton. Cover all the seams with gold braid, and add a narrow band of black velvet ribbon down the centre front edged on either side with gold braid. Now set gold buttons at regular intervals to the centre of the black velvet ribbon.

Join up the five sections which make the back body and the hump: the two body sides in the yellow and red patterned cotton, the two sides to the hump in orange cotton, and the hump itself in the yellow and red patterned cotton. Gather the top of the sides of the hump (X to O) to the sides of the two back bodies. The hump itself when sewn to the orange sides should terminate at O. Then gather or ease the width of the top of the hump (O to O) to the measurement of the back neck. Cover all the seams with gold braid.

The upper legs, both back and front, are of the blue patterned cotton on the insides, and the four outer sections are of the orange-coloured cotton. Cover the seams, both backs and fronts, with the gold braid.

Assemble and sew all front and all back sections together, gathering the front of the body waistline towards the centre front of the leg waistline to give the fullness of the peascod belly when padding. Sew completed front body to completed back body, turn right side out and pad.

Cover the side seams of the body, from shoulder edges to the commencement of the stockings, with bands of red silk ribbon.

Cover the join of stockings to upper legs with the embroidered ribbon, finishing off with a brightly-coloured rosette positioned on the outside of each leg.

Edge the top of the shoes with the brown Russian braid, adding brightly-coloured rosettes to the fronts.

Skirts: Make up the skirts in alternate sections of the orange and blue patterned cottons. Cover all the seams with gold braid, including the fronts and the hem, then line with the bright red cotton. Now gather the top edge of the skirts evenly to the body waistline and sew in position.

Belt: The waistline is finished off with a band of the embroidered ribbon (lined to give it thickness) complete with a brightly-coloured rosette, centred with a small buckle or brooch, at the centre front.

Arms: The fronts of the arms are in the blue patterned cotton and the backs in the orange cotton. Assemble and sew all front and all back sections together. Then sew completed fronts to completed backs, turn right side out and pad. Cover the seams with gold braid, terminating at the wrists.

Add a gathered falling frill of deep gold lace to the join of hands to sleeves, and cover the joins with a band of the red silk ribbon.

Now make up the puff sleeves in the orange-coloured silk and gather the lower edges to bands of the embroidered ribbon (the bands should be lined). Place on the arms, gathering the heads of the sleeves to the tops of the arms, simulating the shape of an armhole. Sew the finished arms firmly to the edge of the shoulders.

Cover the shoulders with epaulettes of rose-red silk (lined with the same material), banded round with bright red cotton, 6mm deep when finished.

Ruff: Take a strip of gold lace (you will need quite a lot) and fold it up and down like a concertina to the depth of the white foundation (lined with the same material). Now, taking the folded lace, follow the same process in making up the ruff as described on p. 58 (le Capitaine) but omit the catching of each pleat on the outside edge. Then place the finished ruff around the neck of the figure, with the ends meeting at the centre back, and firmly sew in position. Finish off by joining the two ends of the gold lace together at the back of the head.

Hat: Make up as described on p. 6. Add a deep gold braid hatband and at the right-hand side a cockade of multicoloured feathers; the base is decorated with a bunch of red silk ribbons and an extravagant brooch or ornament. Do not glue or sew the finished hat to the head.

Head: Make up each ear in two thicknesses of the white cotton and add an interlining of felt to stiffen them. Paint in the features with black, and sew the completed ears to the side seams of the head.

Now position and fix the hat well to the back of the head.

The felt features should next be placed and glued to the head; first the two large beige shapes with the red eyes, then the pink cheeks to below the eyes on either side of the face.

The remaining features, characterising a wicked and malicious look, are all painted in with the black dye or poster colour: the eyelids and pupils, the frown and the arched eyebrows, the sneering smile and the thin up-turned moustaches.

Accessories: A wooden club hangs from a black cord looped over his left wrist and is held menacingly – by glue – in his right hand.

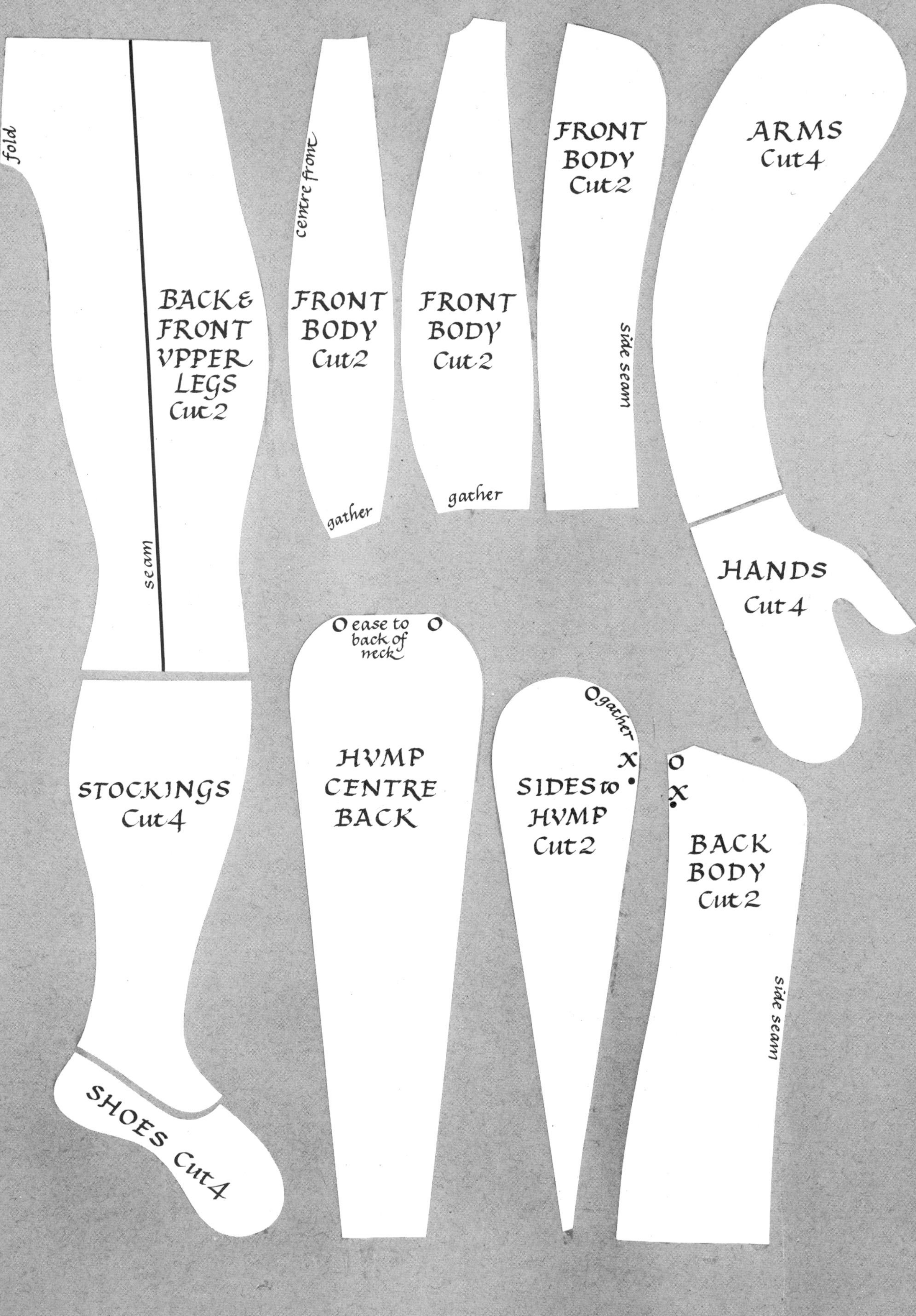

BACK &
FRONT
VPPER
LEGS
Cut 2

fold

centre front

seam

FRONT
BODY
Cut 2

gather

FRONT
BODY
Cut 2

gather

FRONT
BODY
Cut 2

side seam

ARMS
Cut 4

HANDS
Cut 4

STOCKINGS
Cut 4

SHOES Cut 4

HVMP
CENTRE
BACK

O ease to
back of
neck

O

SIDES to
HVMP
Cut 2

O gather

X

O

X

BACK
BODY
Cut 2

side seam

SIDES of CROWN to HAT

BRIM to HAT Cut 2

TOP of HAT

FRONT HEAD
Cut 2

BACK HEAD
Cut 2

CHEEKS
Cut 2

BACK SKIRTS

gather

CB Fold

seam

seam

EPAULETTES Cut 2

FRONT SKIRTS Cut 2

gather

side seam

seam

KNEE & BELT ROSETTES Cut 3

SHOE ROSETTES Cut 2

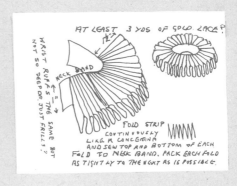

AT LEAST 3 YDS OF GOLD LACE

WRIST RUFFS THE SAME BUT NOT SO DEEP OR JUST FRILLS.

NECK BAND

FOLD STRIP CONTINUOUSLY LIKE A CONCERTINA AND SEW TOP AND BOTTOM OF EACH FOLD TO NECK BAND. PACK EACH FOLD AS TIGHTLY TO THE NEXT AS IS POSSIBLE.

NECK BAND FOUNDATION for RUFF

gather

PUFF SLEEVES Cut 2

gather to band

BAND to PUFF SLEEVES Cut 2

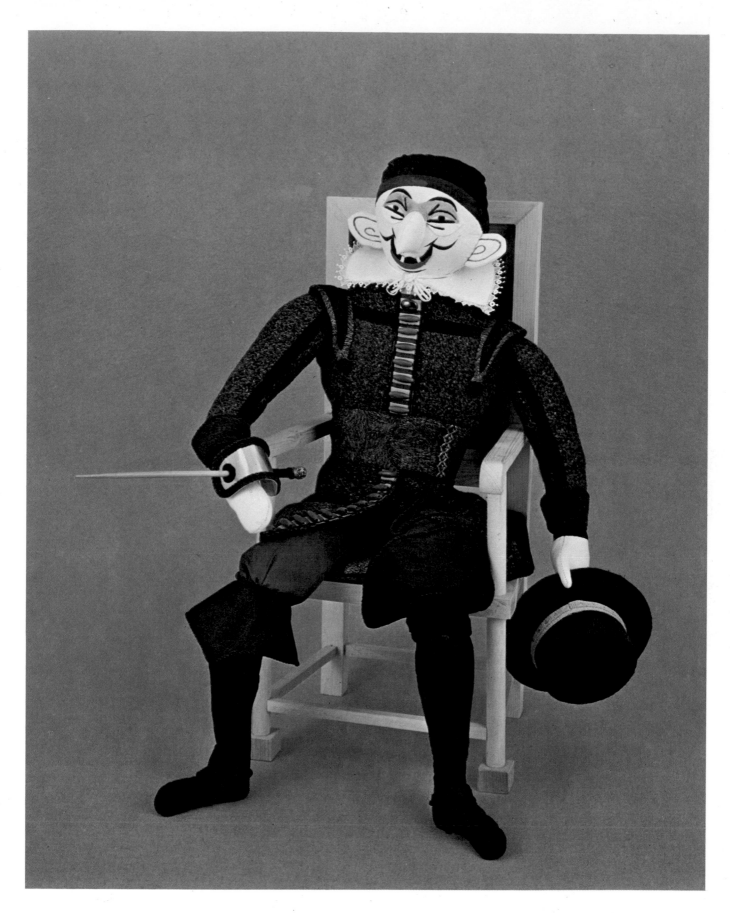

CRISPIN
Based on the portrait of Raymond Poisson by Bonnart

86

CRISPIN

Origins and Development

Like Polichinelle, Crispin is a French addition to the long list of the characters in the Commedia, and there is no evidence that he appeared in Italy. The role was created and made famous by Raymond Poisson. On his death in 1690, the part continued to be played by other Poissons until it disappeared sometime during the middle of the eighteenth century, deteriorating into a very minor servant without the very personal characterisation given to this part by the original Poisson. He belongs to the group of characters who are associated with the military profession, and Duchartre refers to him as the 'son' of Scaramouche. There is one print of a seventeenth-century Scaramouche who looks remarkably like Crispin, though the costume is entirely different. With the little information available much has to be conjectural in establishing the soul of the character, but it is clear that he makes the third, in France, of a group of deformed characters – Crispin, Polichinelle and Pulcinella. This evocative, allusive and charming creature unfortunately had an imbecile face, hunchback and pigeon chest.

The creation of one man, Poisson, his uniqueness echoes our inability to recreate the imagination and skills of many later music-hall performers, or the bizarre characters of early film comedies. Like Fiorilli's Scaramouche, Poisson's Crispin has gone into oblivion.

Role

The costume suggests a rider of horse or a groom, servant, messenger or soldier. Nothing in the scenarios helps to identify his role.

Character

He may well have been a simpleton or 'village idiot'. It is possible that he could neither read or write, learning everything by heart – like well-known little ballads or short verses, and he was also a very poor musician.

The Mask

It seems that Poisson played without a mask, painting his face white with an expression touched with pathos. He has slit eyes, betraying signs of a simpleton, though there is a charm shining through, simple as it may be. His mouth smiles in a full half-moon shape revealing that he has lost most of his teeth. The ears are pointed and sharp. The hair is covered by the traditional skullcap.

Costume

Information is based on the print of Poisson by Bonnart. The style is close to clothes worn by soldiers and horsemen around the middle and latter part of the seventeenth century. Plain and dark in colour, the deep-skirted riding coat is high-waisted and fastened down the front with toggle buttons. The belt is broad with a sword thrust through it. The simple cuffed sleeves terminate at the shoulders with epaulettes. The collar is very large and old-fashioned, belonging to the first quarter of the seventeenth century. It is semicircular in shape, stiffened by means of a *supportasse* and edged with narrow lace – an ideal collar to emphasise his lack of neck and his hunchback. The breeches are full and gathered in at the knee. He wears 'bucket boots' (a clue that he rode horse). The tops of the boots, to protect the upper leg from dirt, are held up to the waistline by cords, but poor Crispin seems only to have concerned himself with fastening up one, as the other hangs down over the lower part of the right leg. The skullcap is black and he carries in his hand a plain lowish-crowned hat with a medium-sized brim.

Movement

He was probably ungainly and unco-ordinated. Perhaps Poisson, who was very popular with Parisian audiences, had a special 'act' of his own – more as an observer in the comedies than participator, rather like Harpo in the Marx brothers team?

Speech, Voice and Other Skills

This is best summed up by a charming verse beneath the Bonnart engraving:

> *Crispin, dont tu vois la figure,*
> *Est un pauvre musicien;*
> *Qui n'entend rien en tablature*
> *Si ce n'est qu'il entonne bien.*

> (Crispin, whose face you see within,
> Musicians say is poor;
> The written note means naught to him,
> Unless he's heard it all before.)

Materials

Select your own choice of materials for the costume for this character, bearing in mind that they should be textured and dark.

Cotton: white (head, ears, nose, collar, hands, upper legs to kneebands)
orange striped with brown (body, skirts)
black (skullcap)
Cotton corduroy: brown (cuffs, epaulettes)
Flecked tweed: brown (body, skirts, arms)
Silk: richly textured black and gold (belt, edging and lining for the epaulettes)
black/purple shot silk (boots, skirt lining)
brown (breeches, cuff linings, belt lining)
Wool: black (kneebands)
Ribbon: black (body, arms) 12mm
indigo blue (skullcap) 12mm
Narrow lace: white (collar) 10mm
Braid: fancy patterned (belt) 12mm
brown Russian (boots, body, skirts, belt)
white Russian (collar)
beige (hat) 12mm
Silk cord: (boots, cuffs, sword)
Felt: brown (hat)
grey (face)
white (face)
black (face)
red (face)

Dye: black (face features)
Wooden toggle buttons: (body, skirts)
Four brown cloth-covered buttons: (epaulettes)
Chopstick: (sword blade)
Ornamental knob: (pommel to sword)
Gold thin metal or card: (sword hilt)
Card: (hat, collar)
Padding

Making

Basic Figure: First sew a band of the black cotton ribbon high across the chest of the front body. Then add a 25mm band of the orange and brown striped cotton down the centre front of the body and edge it all round with the brown Russian braiding. Sew the centre backs of the hump together and join the base of the hump to the back body; cover this join with a band of the black cotton ribbon. Now gather (O to O) at the top edge of the hump to the same measurement as the width of the back neck; gather (A to X) on either side of the back body so that the measurement (from B to O) is exactly the same as the measurement of the front body (B to O).

Assemble and sew all front and all back sections together. Sew completed front body to completed back body, turn right side out and pad: push as much padding into the chest area as possible.

Cover the join of the black skullcap to head with indigo blue cotton ribbon. Assemble, make up and pad the arms and cover the seams down to the hands, including around the wrists, with the black cotton ribbon. Make up the cuffs in the brown corduroy (lined with brown silk) and edge all round with the brown silk cord. Now sew the cuffs to the top edges of the black wristbands with the open sides of the cuffs positioned on the outside of the arms. Do *not* attach the arms to the body.

Breeches: Make up according to pattern. Gather and sew the waistline of the breeches evenly to the waistline of the figure. Gather the hems of the legs to the top edges of the black wool kneebands.

Skirts: Make up and line with the black/purple shot silk. Add a 25mm band of the orange and brown striped cotton down the edge of the right front, and edge it all round with the brown Russian braid. Now form a box pleat at the centre back (see pattern) and ease and sew the top of the skirts to the waistline. *Make sure* that the line of the right-hand side of the front of the skirts follows through the orange and brown striped cotton band on the body.

Belt: Make up in the textured black and gold silk (lined with brown silk) and edge all round with the brown Russian braid. Position the belt high to the waistline of the figure, joining it together towards the front of the body on the left-hand side. (Use the line marked 'position for braid' on the pattern for the join, thus leaving the curved end of the belt loose and flapping.) Sew a band of fancy braid to the outside of the belt corresponding with the line of this join.

Buttons: Now sew wooden toggle buttons at regular intervals right down the centre front of the coat.

Boots: Line the boot tops with the same black/purple shot silk and edge all round with the brown silk cord. Sew the lower edges of the boot tops to the top edges of the black wool kneebands, making sure that the pointed tops are centred to the front of the legs. Let the right-hand boot top fall down but hold up the left with a loop of brown cord, sewn to the point, and attach it to the waistline.

Make up the boot fronts in the black/purple shot silk (lining them with the same material) and edge all round with the brown Russian braid; position and sew them across the insteps. Finish off with a band of brown Russian braid placed around the ankles and over the boot fronts.

Arms and Epaulettes: Now sew the arms firmly to the edge of the shoulders. Cover the shoulders with epaulettes of brown cotton corduroy (lined with the textured black and gold silk), banded all round with the textured black and gold silk 6mm deep when finished. Terminate both the backs and fronts of the epaulettes with small brown cloth-covered buttons.

Collar: Check the shape of the neckline of the collar to the neckline shape of the figure. The collar should fit *exactly*; the pattern may need reshaping depending on how the neck has been padded. When the neck edge exactly fits, cut the collar out of card (leaving A on the pattern open) and cover it, back and front, with white cotton. Decorate the outside perimeter with a narrow band of white lace.

Now place around the neck of the figure, high at the back, and firmly sew or glue in position, joining up A to A. Cover the neck edge with white Russian braid, adding a bow of loops of the same braid to the centre of the throat.

Hat: Make up in brown felt as described on page 6, lining the inside of the crown with the same material. Add a hatband of beige braid to complete, and place the hat in the left hand when the figure is finished.

Head: Make up each ear in two thicknesses of white cotton and interline with felt to stiffen them. Paint the features in black and sew the finished ears to the side seams of the head, commencing at the front termination of the skullcap. Make up the nose, pad it with soft cottonwool, and sew in position.

Now place and glue the felt features; grey felt above eyes, white eyes, black crescent-shaped open mouth with two white teeth, and the lower lip in red. All the other features are painted in black; eyebrows, upper and lower eyelids, little beady eyes, the chin and the cheeks.

Sword: Make up as described on page 58 (le Capitaine), adding two thicknesses of the brown silk cord around the edge of the gold hilt. Place in Crispin's right hand and glue firmly.

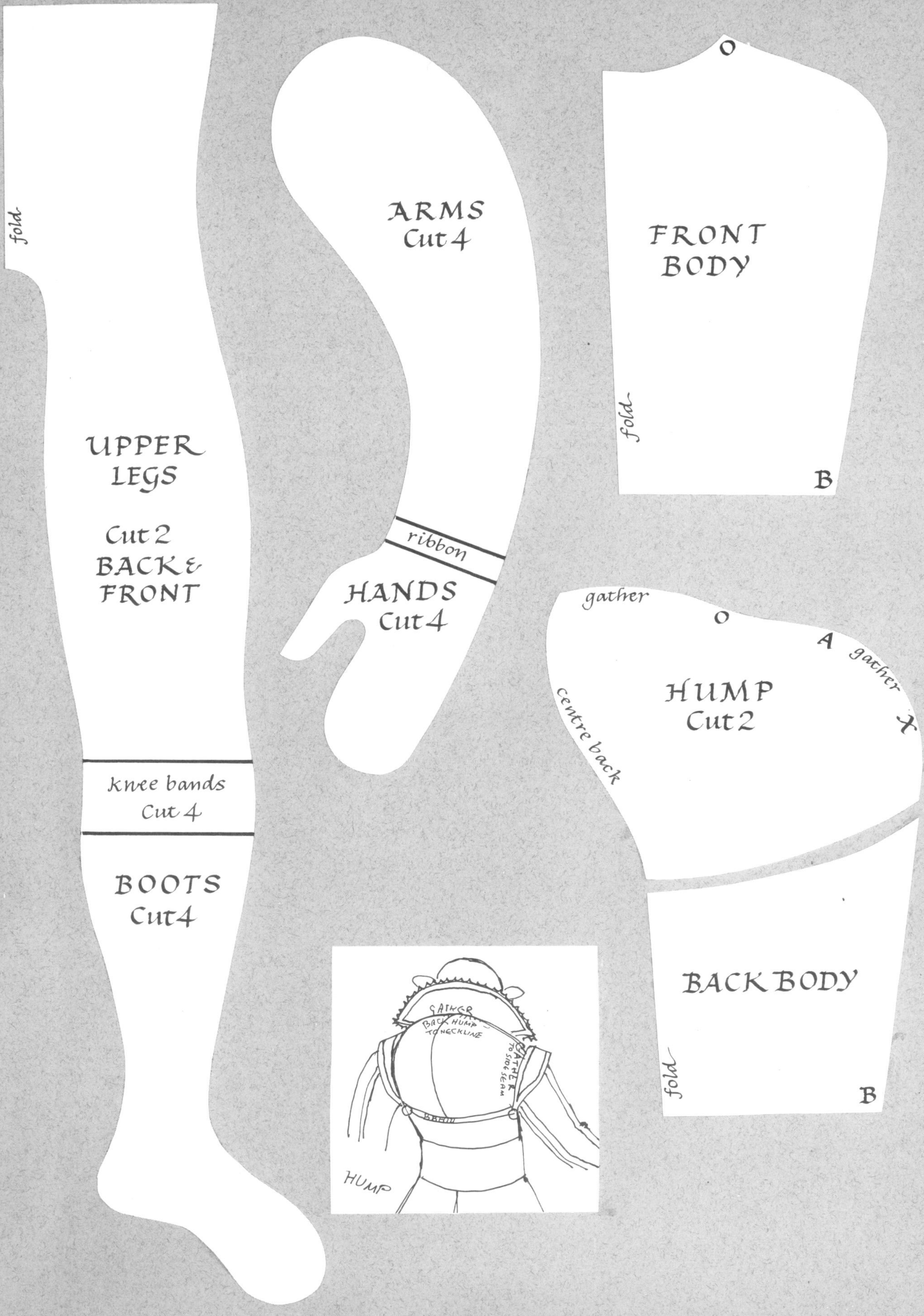

fold

UPPER
LEGS

Cut 2
BACK &
FRONT

knee bands
Cut 4

BOOTS
Cut 4

ARMS
Cut 4

ribbon

HANDS
Cut 4

FRONT
BODY

fold

O

B

gather

O

A gather

HUMP
Cut 2

centre back

BACK BODY

fold

B

GATHER
BACK HUMP
TO NECKLINE

GATHER
TO SIDE SEAM

HUMP

BACK of
SKULLCAP

fold

BACK
NECK

fold

FRONT of
SKULLCAP

fold

FRONT
FACE

fold

FRONT SKIRTS
Cut 2

side seam

gather

fold

BREECHES
Cut 2
BACK & FRONT

gather

box *pleat*

BACK
SKIRTS

side seam

fold

CUFFS
Cut 2

BRIM TO HAT Cut 2

EPAULETTES Cut 2

GREY.

RED

BE IN SYMPATHY WITH HIM ✻ NOT JUST A GROTESQUE

TOP of HAT

B E L T

NOSE

fold

SIDES of CROWN to HAT

BOOT TOP Cut 2

position
for braid

COLLAR Cut 2

A | A

BOOT
FRONTS Cut 2

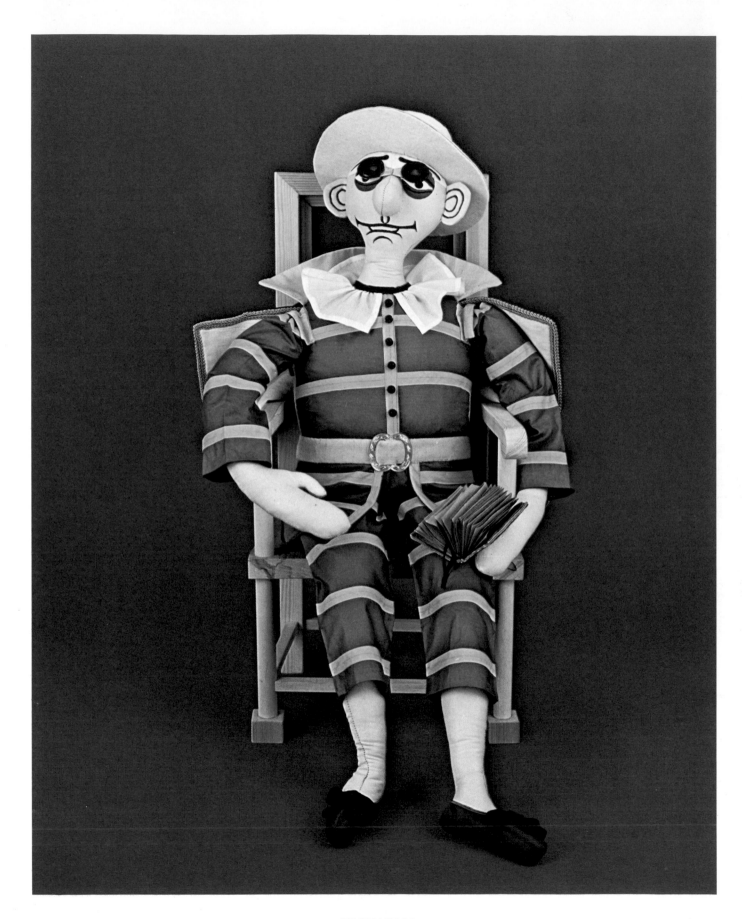

TARTAGLIA
Based on a lithograph by Maurice Sand in '*Masques et bouffons*', 1862

TARTAGLIA

Origins and Development

Neapolitan in origin, this role like so many of the other characters in the Commedia can be traced back to the ancient *Phylakes* and the Atellan farces. He is a pedant and a philosopher who loves long speeches and his own importance. A very strange character, he plays a relatively minor role and has no place in the scenarios. Tartaglia altered very little in his history, but he did become less grotesque and fat with the passing of time. From the information available there is little evidence that he gained any popularity in France, though we do know that he appeared in countries outside of Italy which was his true home. He is included in this group of figures because of his very strong individual characterisation and his very distinctive costume.

Role

He frequently accompanies the Doctor, acting as a comical butt in their various plots and intrigues. In some scenarios he had a wife and family.

Character

A farcical, stammering and very corpulent notary or some other member of the legal profession. At times he appeared as an apothecary. He has little or no sense of humour, and is extremely pompous – and also very short-sighted. It is possible that he had many similar characteristics to those of the late W.C. Fields.

The Mask

Tartaglia does not wear the mask but whitens his face and wears a white skullcap giving the appearance of baldness. The facial expression is smug and akin to a frog, with his slit eyes trying to focus behind enormous circular blue or green-tinted spectacles. His nose is bulbous and coarse and he has a long sneering smile on his mouth.

Costume

His dress is in green, banded at regular intervals with bright yellow. The deep-skirted jacket is belted high over his great belly, and is buttoned down the front; the neckline is finished off with a gathered, falling, open collar of white; the sleeves are open at the wrists. His shortish trousers are banded in yellow like his jacket. The knee-length collared cloak, the stockings and broad-brimmed hat are all in white. The trousers usually have pockets placed high in the side seams, into which he thrusts his hands – a pose to emphasise his corpulence and smugness.

Movement

May be slow in his walk with his belly thrust forward; or, like the Doctor, he may have walked with tiny mincing steps with his great body swaying to and fro?

Speech, Voice and Other Skills

Stuttering and his love of long speeches were his chief weapons to gain a laugh. To the characters appearing with him in his scenes, his slow, precise choice of words must have brought tedium, boredom and frustration! Tartaglia often appeared in disguise, usually as a Greek or Roman god or goddess, 'sending-up' the characters in the tragedies, ballets, and court masques which were at the height of their popularity in France and Italy. In the stage directions from one scenario we read 'Enter Tartaglia dressed as Venus'.

Materials

Cotton: natural coloured (head, nose, ears, arms, legs)
    green glazed (body, skirts, sleeves, trousers)
    fine white (collar)
    white (cloak lining, skullcap, cloak collar)
    bright green (face features)
Silk: dark green (cloak)
    yellow (belt, cloak collar lining, epaulettes)
    brown (shoes)
Felt: white (hat, eyes)
    narrow strip of dark green (neckline) 6mm
Ribbon: black (shoes) 12mm
    cream (hat) 12mm
Braid: green Russian (shoes)
    fancy yellow (cloak) 6mm
Bias binding: yellow (body, skirts, sleeves, trousers) 12mm
Simple black buttons: (body)
Large buckle: (belt)
Dye: black (face features)
Card: (hat)
Two tapwashers 25mm across and two metal,
    circular, beer-can openers: (spectacles)
A book
Padding

Making

First sew in place (as marked on the patterns) all the yellow bands of bias binding to the two front body parts, the two back body parts, the fronts and backs of the trousers, the sleeves, and the skirts – which are all cut from the green glazed cotton. When making up it is *essential* to match the bands seam to seam, as for example the inner and outer seams of the trousers.

Basic Figure: Sew up the two fronts of the body, adding a narrow band of the yellow bias binding with the small black buttons set at regular intervals down the centre front. Then sew up the two backs of the body. Assemble and sew all back and all front sections together, easing both the front body waistline and the back to fit the leg waistline. Sew completed front body to completed back body, turn right side out and pad.

Edge the top of the shoes with the green Russian braid, adding little bows of black ribbon to the fronts.

Assemble, make up and pad the arms. Then make up the green sleeves, hemming the bottom edges; place on the arms, and gather the heads to the tops of the arms, simulating the shape of an armhole. When finished, the seams of the sleeves should balance with the inner seams of the arms. Do *not* attach the completed arms to the body.

Trousers: Make up the trousers, hemming the ends of the

legs. Place on the figure, gathering the waistline evenly to fit the body waistline, and sew in position. Make sure that the side seams of the trousers correspond with the outside seams of the legs.

Skirts: Line the skirts in the same glazed green cotton, adding a band of the yellow bias binding to the front edges. Attach the top of the skirts to the body waistline, allowing a 20mm gap at the centre front. (The top edge of the skirts will require some gathering, particularly at the back, to fit the figure.)

Belt: The waistline is finished off with a yellow silk belt, lined with the same material, complete with buckle.

Neckline: Hem the collar, of white fine cotton, then gather the top edge to the neckline of the body, leaving a gap of 12mm at the centre front. Finish off the neck edge with a 6mm band of dark green felt.

Arms and Epaulettes: Now sew the arms firmly to the edge of the shoulders. Cover the shoulders with epaulettes of yellow silk, lined with the same material.

Hat: Make up the hat in white felt as described on page 6. In this instance it is *not* necessary to oversew the outer circumference of the brim. Simply trim the edge of the three thicknesses of white felt and card. (No turning allowance, therefore, is necessary, but all three thicknesses should be firmly glued together.) Finish off by adding a band of cream ribbon to the base of the crown. Do not fix the hat to the head.

Head: Make up the nose, pad with soft cottonwool and sew it in position immediately below the edge of the white skullcap. Next, make up each ear in two thicknesses of material with an interlining of felt to stiffen them. Then paint the ear features in black. When completed sew the ears to the side seams of the head.

Now glue or sew the hat, well to the back of the head.

Glue two bright green circles of cotton to either side of the nose with the tops of the circles just covering the commencement of the skullcap; next, glue the white felt eyes to the centre of the circles. All the features are painted in black – eyes, eyelids, eyebrows, long sneering smile, mouth and chins.

Cloak: Line the dark green silk cloak with white cotton and band all round with narrow fancy braid. The white cotton collar is lined with the yellow silk. Oversew the edge of the neckline of the collar to the cloak, centring it to the longer edge. Now place the cloak on the figure, catching it on either side of the shoulders at the commencement of the epaulettes to keep it in position.

Spectacles: Here you must use imagination. The spectacles for the sculpture were made up from two circular beer-can openers, glued together with the epoxy glue; to the top surface of each circle was added a 25mm tap-washer, painted black. The same glue was also used to fix the finished spectacles firmly to the top of the nose.

Accessories: To emphasise his profession, give Tartaglia a law-book to hold in his hand.

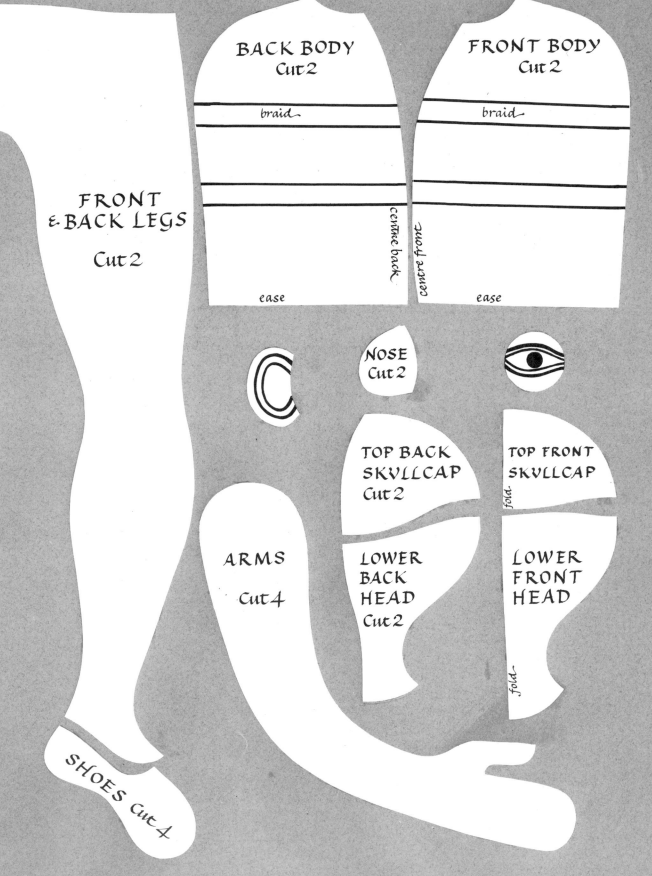

FRONT
& BACK LEGS

Cut 2

fold

BACK BODY
Cut 2

braid

centre back

ease

FRONT BODY
Cut 2

braid

centre front

ease

NOSE
Cut 2

TOP BACK
SKULLCAP
Cut 2

LOWER
BACK
HEAD
Cut 2

TOP FRONT
SKULLCAP

fold

LOWER
FRONT
HEAD

fold

ARMS

Cut 4

SHOES Cut 4

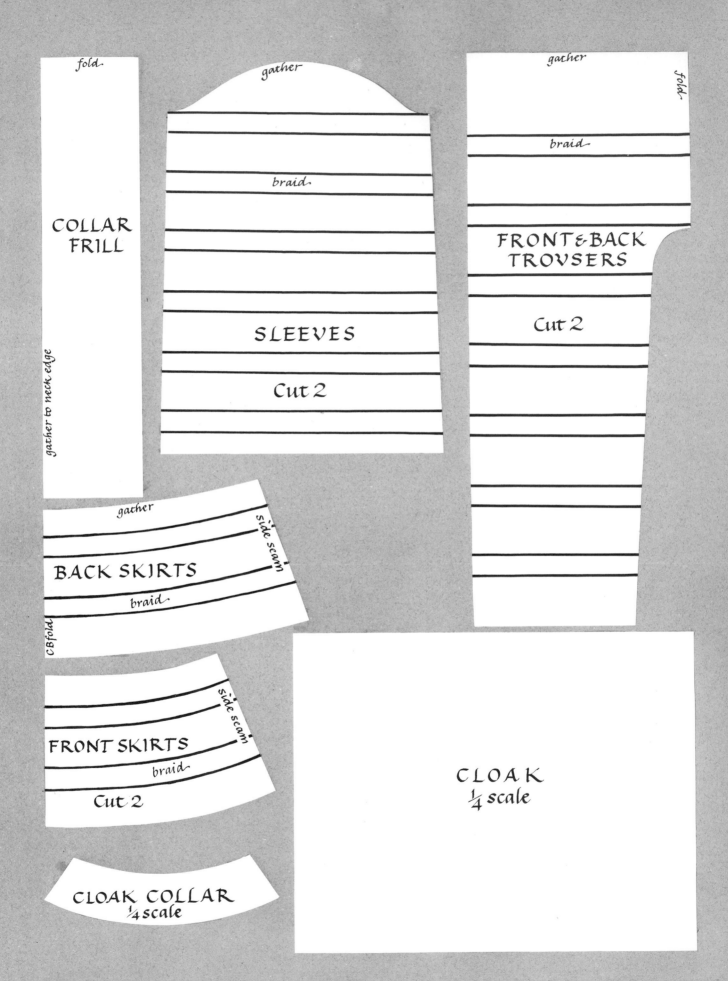

TARTALIA

GREEN
BANDED WITH
YELLOW.

GLASSES-
BLUE

1. RESHAPE BODY
3. SHORTEN LEGS
2. FATTEN FACE
4. CURVE ARMS

2 FRONT

Fat
midwais

Hands in
pockets

A BOOK
TO CARRY.

HEAD BROADER
BODY ROUND
LEGS SHORT
ARMS CURVE

TARTALIA.

BUCKLE *
GLASSES?
2 BEER CAN PULLS.

FRONTAL FACE
NOSE AND FACE

TOP of HAT

SIDES of CROWN to HAT

fold

BELT Cut 2

EPAULETTES Cut 4

BRIM TO HAT Cut 2

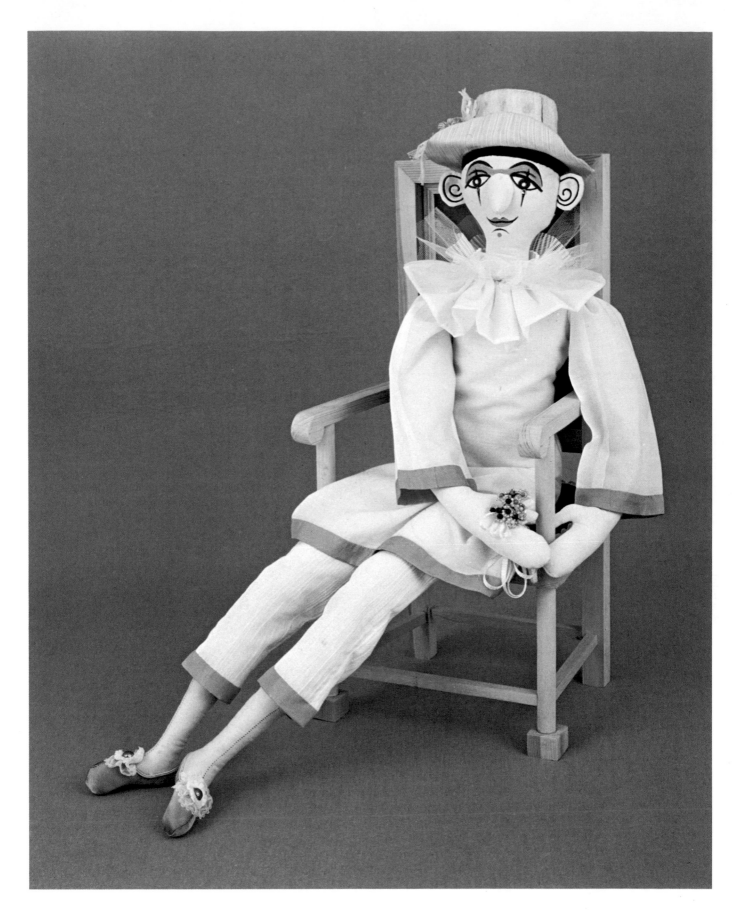

PIERROT
Freely based on several paintings and prints of the second half of the seventeenth century

PIERROT

Origins and Development

His name (French) comes from the Italian Pedrolino, Piero or Pierotto. One of the most sensitive and charming of the masks, he makes his appearance in Italy in the sixteenth century; but from the beginning of the eighteenth century onwards his popularity became equal to that of Arlequin. One of the most famous interpreters of the part was the Ferrarese actor Guiseppe Geratoni, who appeared in Paris for the first time in 1763.

By the nineteenth century Pierrot's character became very sentimental when appearing in the Harlequinades. Later he gave his name to the Pierrot troupes which became very popular in England at the beginning of the twentieth century and played at many seaside resorts right up to the outbreak of World War II. The Pierrot in the Harlequinade and Pierrots in the Pierrot troupes based their costumes on Pagliaccio, a minor character appearing as a Prologue, or as an acrobat or a coarse comedian, in the Commedia. His costume rarely varied – a long white floppy tunic, with black pom-poms in the front, and with very long sleeves hanging down over his hands; wide trousers; a whitened face (sometimes he wore the half-mask or domino); a black or white skullcap; a tall white conical shaped hat with a very narrow brim; and a deep white gathered frill at the neck. Pagliaccio achieved permanent fame when Leoncavallo gave him his dramatic Prologue in the opera *I Pagliacci*.

Role

A dreamy, sad, lovesick young servant or valet who is frequently punished for mistakes he never commits. He is tender and trustworthy and full of charm, always willing to come to the assistance of others; but he has a naïve sense of mischief, often miming the happiness or sadness of the characters he appears with. He enjoys re-enacting and commenting on their situations, making full use of contact with his audience in the process. Usually played as an isolated and lonely character, he is at times accompanied by a young girl-servant with whom he is desperately but forlornly in love.

Character

His age is difficult to determine; he is timid and awkward in his relationships and behaviour towards his fellow men. He possesses a simple elegance, but is more associated with the country-side than with the town. Very sensitive, Pierrot always attempts to be merry in the company of others but sheds buckets of tears when alone. When admonished or punished or witnessing the misfortunes of others he may also burst into tears – devouring great quantities of food at the same time. It is very important for the actor interpreting this role to remember that his performance should make the audience laugh directly at *him*, and not necessarily at his place in the plot.

The Mask

Pierrot does not wear the mask, and conceals his hair beneath a black skullcap. The expression should be melancholy, yet constantly changing when imitating the situations of others. He paints his face white.

Costume

Soft and all in white, though some interpreters introduced touches of pale blue. The costume is not so loose and floppy as the costume worn by either Pulcinella or Pagliaccio, and at the time of Louis XIV it became very elegant. He wore a white, slightly waisted knee-length tunic with long open sleeves. The white trousers were somewhat short. Over his skullcap he wore a straw or felt hat with a smallish or sometimes wide upcurved brim, and around his neck a full and gathered soft ruff or collar of one or many layers. The loose tunic could be buttoned through and was at times belted. The shoes were soft and of a pale colour, with simple or no trimmings.

Movement

Could be either very awkward or elegant according to the situation as outlined in the scenario: he could change in a moment from a mechanical stiffness like a scarecrow or a puppet to balletic movement, liquid and lyrical in sensitivity. The facial expression, as already mentioned, was equally mobile and changeable as the rest of his body.

Speech, Voice and Other Skills

Often silent, his skill lay in the art of mime, mimicry and dance. Contemporary examples have been seen in the great skills and art of Marcel Marceau and Jean-Louis Barrault (the latter particularly in the classic film *les Enfants du Paradis*). He sings well and plays various musical instruments, but it was with his balletic skill of movement and sense of rhythm in his interpretation of fear, naughtiness, falling on the floor in a flood of tears and imitating the emotions of the other characters – love, unrequited love, laughter, anger and frustration – that he achieved his great popularity.

Materials

Cotton: white (head, ears, nose, arms, body)
soft white (tunic, sleeves, trousers)
semi-transparent white (neck frills)
white net and tarlatan (neck frills)
black (skullcap)
natural colour (legs)
Silk: pale blue (tunic, trousers)
pinky brown (shoes)
raw silk, natural colour (hat)
Lace of various widths: white (hat, shoes)
Braid: yellow Russian (shoes)
Silk cord: grey (hat)
Felt: grey (face)
Dye: black (face)
pink (face)
blue (face)
Two gold buttons: (shoes)
Two silver sequins: (eyes)
White ribbon streamers
Artificial flowers: (hat and carried posy)
Card: (hat)
Padding

Making

Basic Figure: Assemble and sew all front and all back sections together. Sew completed front body to completed back body, turn right side out and pad. Edge the top of the shoes with yellow Russian braid, adding small lace rosettes, centred with a small gold button, to the fronts.

Assemble, make up and pad the arms but do *not* attach them to the body.

Trousers: Make up according to pattern, adding a band of pale blue to the leg ends. Gather and sew the waistline of the trousers to the waistline of the figure. Make sure that the side seams of the trousers match the side seams of the body.

Tunic: Make up according to patterns, leaving the shoulder seams open, and add a band of pale blue to the hem. Now place on the figure and sew up the shoulder seams. Lastly sew the neckline to the neckline of the figure.

Arms and Sleeves: Make up the sleeves, adding a band of pale blue to the ends. Next gather the heads of the sleeves. Now slip the arms into the sleeves, making sure that the inside seams of the arms match the inside seams of the sleeves. Sew the gathered head of the sleeves to the top of the arms, to simulate the shape of an armhole. Then firmly sew the arms, complete with sleeves, to the body, commencing at the edge of the shoulders. The tunic is now finished save for the neck frill.

Neck Edge: Make up the neck frill with each layer (3 or more) in a different semi-transparent white fabric to create a variety of textures. Hem if necessary, place them all together, gather the top edge to the same measurement as the neckline of the tunic and sew in position.

Hat: Make up the hat as described on page 6. Decorate the base of the crown with a thickish grey silk cord, and add to one side a small bunch of yellow flowers (choose country flowers) decorated with a small cockade and streamers of various widths of white lace. Lastly turn up the front of the brim, attaching it to the front of the crown. Do not glue or sew the hat to the head until the nose and the ears have been completed.

Head: Make up the nose, pad with soft cottonwool and sew in position. Next, make up the ears in two thicknesses of material with an interlining of felt to stiffen them. Then paint in the features with black. When completed, sew the ears to the side seams of the head, commencing at the front termination of the black skullcap.

Now firmly fix the hat in position.

All the features on the face are painted except for the grey upper lids to the eyes, which are cut out of felt and glued to the head. The eyes are blue, the mouth pink, with the rest of the features and the expression – which should be gentle and melancholy – painted in black save for a little pink dot at the centre of the chin. Lastly, add a silver sequin to the centre of the lower edge of each eye to suggest that Pierrot is on the verge of tears.

Accessories: Place in one hand a little bunch of flowers accompanied with streamers of white ribbon.

BACK & FRONT
LEGS
Cut 2

BACK BODY   FRONT BODY

fold   fold

ARMS
Cut 4

BRIM to HAT Cut 2

TOP of HAT

SHOES Cut 4

ROSETTES
Cut 2

SIDES of CROWN to HAT

NECK FRILLS

DEPTH of THIRD LAYER

fold

DEPTH of SECOND LAYER

DEPTH of TOP LAYER

gather to neckline

NOSE

fold

BACK TOP
PART of
SKVLLCAP
Cut 2

gather

fold

LOWER BACK
PART of
SKVLLCAP
Cut 2

BACK & FRONT.
TROVSERS
Cut 2

BACK
of
NECK

fold

FRONT
SKVLLCAP

fold

PIERROT.

VIOLETS

FULL LENGTH
ARMS

FRONT
FACE

fold

TVNIC SLEEVES
Cut 2

gather

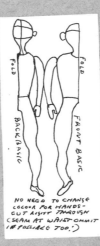

NO NEED TO CHANGE
COLOUR FOR HANDS-
CUT RIGHT THROUGH
(SEAM AT WAIST OMMIT
IF POSSIBLE TOO.)

TVNIC FRONT

fold

TVNIC BACK

fold

MEZZETINO
Freely based on the paintings of Watteau and earlier prints

MEZZETINO

Origins and Development

Appearing in Italy during the sixteenth century he was sometimes called Mezetin (= half and half), a deceiver and deceived. One of the many servant/valet roles, the part was originally linked to the mask of Brighella, but by the second half of the seventeenth century his character, temperament, and costume changed. Angelo Constantini (1654-1729) from Verona established a new Mezzetino, just as Tiberio Fiorilli created a new Scaramouche. Constantini performed in many of the courts of Europe including Spain, Poland, and France where he became a great success, and was also a favourite subject for artists and painters, among them Watteau and Bonnart. Molière and Marivaux used and adapted this character for many of their plays.

Role

An elegant valet as played by Constantini. Often acting as a companion to Arlequin, he enjoyed the fun of messing things up within the plot as outlined in the scenario. Like many of the other servants he accepted bribes, and though seemingly honest to his master, could intrigue with others against him from time to time. Sometimes he had a wife who deceived him; then he would also deceive her, flirting with young girls or handsome women (often smug and conceited in doing so).

Character

The charm of a young man very sure of himself and well aware of his attractions where women were concerned! Naughty but not cruel, he is very clever at manipulating situations to suit himself.

The Mask

Constantini never played wearing the mask. He appears in his portraits as a man of sensitive features.

Costume

Originally Mezzetino wore a costume similar to those worn by the slaves in the old Roman comedies – a very loose-fitting tunic, wide trousers, short cape, a long pointed beak-brimmed hat, and he carried a wooden sword. Constantini established the new dress of red-and-white striped material. As a servant he wore the typical full beret falling down to the shoulders at the back. The tunic was of soft material, buttoned through the centre fronts with the skirts cut to knee length or a little shorter. A sash holds the tunic in at the waist. Epaulettes hide the join of the fullish sleeves to the shoulders, and the neck and wrists are finished off with soft frills or a little collar and cuffs. Full breeches of the same material as the tunic are gathered in at the knees and held in place by elegant ties. The stockings are of a delicate colour, and he wears well-fitting soft shoes. The cape, with a collar, is of soft silk and is either short (hip-length) or terminates at the knees. In portraits he is rarely seen without his guitar or mandolin, with ribbon streamers flowing from the instrument.

Movement

Gentle and more courtly than most of the other servants. He dances well.

Speech, Voice and Other Skills

Articulate and cunning, and conceited in his use of words. He had a good singing voice and was an accomplished musician. Many of the early scenarios required him to perform in disguise during the action, usually in the shape of a grotesque female; and it is most probable that he was a very popular entertainer during the *entre'actes*, with his songs.

Materials

Cotton: natural colour (head, nose, arms, body through to stockings)
    grey (cloak collar)
    soft striped multi-colour, including red and white (tunic, sleeves, skirts, breeches, beret)
    pink (stockings)
Silk: pale yellow (sash, kneebands, skirt lining, shoe and knee rosettes)
    beige (shoes)
    pale orange (cloak)
    pale green (cloak collar lining, epaulettes)
    pink (beret)
    bright orange (guitar)
    brown (epaulettes)
Brocade: (guitar)
Lurex: black striped with gold (guitar)
Voile: pale green patterned white (collar, cuffs)
Narrow lace: beige (cuffs) 6mm
Braid: yellow Russian (shoes)
Ribbon: multi-colours (guitar) 10mm
    narrow pink (epaulettes, skirts) 6mm
Suede: pale blue (neck, cuffs) 6mm
Sequins: deep rose-red (tunic, sleeves, skirts, breeches)
Four buttons or ornaments: (knee ties, shoes)
Felt: white (eyes)
    grey (face features)
    black (guitar)
    brown (guitar)
    yellow (basis for hair)
Jute: yellow (hair)
Dye: black (face features)
    dark green (eyes)
    deep rose-pink (mouth)
Semicircular dowel rod: (guitar)
Card: (guitar)
Padding

Making

Basic Figure: Assemble and sew all front and all back sections together. Sew completed front body to completed back body, turn right side out and pad. Edge the top of the shoes with yellow Russian braid, adding yellow silk rosettes centred with an ornamental button to the fronts.

Assemble, make up and pad the arms, but do *not* attach them yet to the body.

Before making up the tunic and the breeches, sew bands of rose-coloured sequins set at regular intervals down the length of the sleeves, the tunic and its skirts, and the breeches.

Breeches: Make up according to pattern. Gather and sew the waistline of the breeches to the waistline of the figure; do the same with the ends of the legs, gathering and sewing them to the line of the top of the stockings. Cover this edge with the kneebands, softly pleated horizontally to decrease the width of the pattern. Lastly, finish off the joins on the outside seams of the legs with yellow silk rosettes each centred with an ornamental button.

Tunic: Make up according to patterns, leaving the shoulder seams as yet unsewn. Place on the figure, sew up the shoulder seams, and sew the neckline to the neckline of the figure. Gather the waistline to the waistline of the figure and sew in position, making sure that the side seams of the tunic correspond with the side seams of the body.

Skirts: Make up the closed skirts according to the pattern, and line with the yellow silk. Edge the hem with narrow pink ribbon. Now gather the top edge of the skirts evenly to the waistline of the figure and sew in position.

Waist Sash: First hem all patterns that go to make up the sash: the sash itself, the sash ends, the simulated sash bow, and the tie. Now softly pleat the sash horizontally to reduce its width to 44mm, and sew it firmly to the figure so as to cover the edges of tunic top and skirts. The join should occur on the left-hand side about 25mm in from the side seam. The sash bow is formed by joining the sides (A to A) to the centre (B). Softly pleat line B to the width of the finished sash. Then vertically pleat and place the simulated tie around the centre of the bow, joining up the tie (A to A) at the lower edge of the bow. Sew the bow in position over the join of the sash. Lastly, gather the tops of the sash ends and sew them to the lower edge of the simulated tie.

Arms and Sleeves: Make up the sleeves, place on the arms, and gather the lower edges to the wrists. Now gather and sew the heads of the sleeves to the tops of the arms, simulating the shape of an armhole. Make up and edge the tops of the voile cuffs with narrow lace, and, gathering the lower edges, sew them to the wrist lines. Cover the joins of cuffs to sleeves with narrow bands of pale blue suede (glueing is preferable to sewing).

Sew the finished arms firmly to the edge of the shoulders. Cover the shoulders with epaulettes of pale green silk lined with the same material, banded on the outside edges with the brown silk 12mm deep when finished, and all round with the narrow pink ribbon.

Collar: Make up in the same material as the cuffs but do not edge with lace. After hemming each tier, join them together at the neck edge, gathering the collar to fit the neckline of the tunic; then sew in position. Finish off by covering the join of the collar to neck with a narrow strip of the pale blue suede, using glue.

Hat: Make up the rim to the beret in heavy pink silk, stiffening the back with felt. Gather the top part of the beret evenly to the top edge of the beret rim. Now leave the hat until the head is complete save for eyes and mouth and painted features.

Head: First, glue the jute to the front of the head, terminating the process according to the line on the pattern. Then make up the side and back hair, sticking the jute in loops to a narrow band of felt. Cut the lower edges of the loops and unravel the jute to form loose curls; glue the felt edge to the sides and back of the head, high enough to be just hidden when the beret is placed in position. The finished result will need trimming.

Now make up the nose, pad with soft cottonwool, and sew in position.

The beret can now be sewn or glued to the head. Depending on the finished shape of the head, the lower edges of the beret may need to be eased to fit. As with Arlequin, add some soft padding to the inside of the beret to control its shape and to give extra bulk to the back of the head.

The eyes cut from white felt, but with the upper eyelids in grey, are then placed and glued in position. The pupils are painted in green, and the mouth in a deep rose-pink. All the other features – the smile, eyebrows and eyelids – are in black. The figure is now complete save for the cloak and the guitar.

Cloak: Cut from the soft orange silk and carefully hem all round. The collar of grey cotton is lined with the pale green silk. When completed it should be positioned to the centre of the top edge of the cloak and oversewn to it. Place on the figure, catching it on either shoulder at the commencement of the epaulettes to keep it in position.

Accessories: The guitar is made up in exactly the same way as Brighella's (see page 22). The top and lower surfaces of the instrument are covered in a brocade to simulate marquetry, and the sides are of heavy bright orange silk; the fingerboard of semicircular dowel rod is covered with the striped Lurex, and the guitar face is finished off with a circle of black felt and edged all round with a narrow strip of brown. The flowing streamers of ribbon should echo the general colour-scheme of the costume.

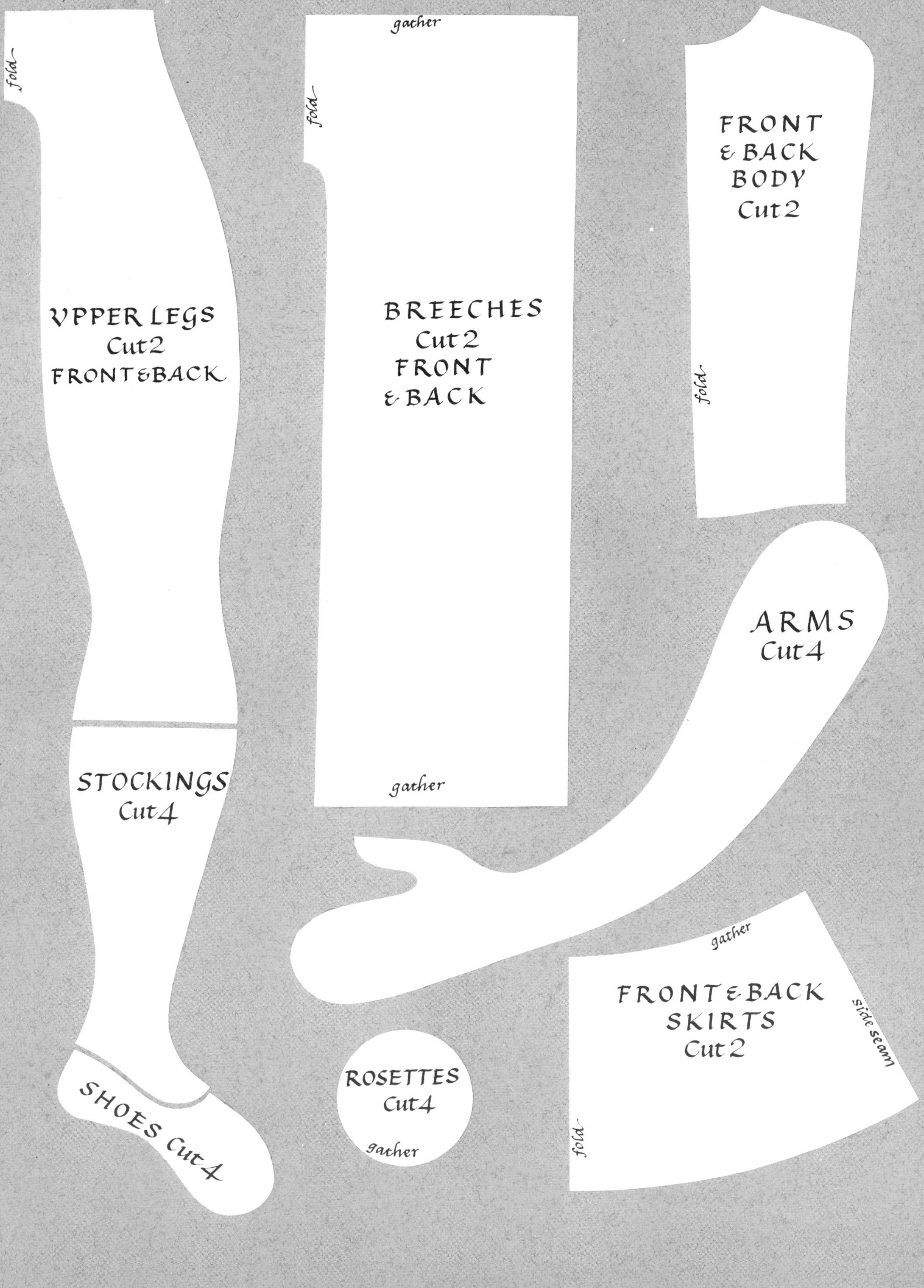

fold

UPPER LEGS
Cut 2
FRONT & BACK

STOCKINGS
Cut 4

SHOES Cut 4

gather

fold

BREECHES
Cut 2
FRONT
& BACK

gather

ROSETTES
Cut 4

gather

FRONT
& BACK
BODY
Cut 2

fold

ARMS
Cut 4

gather

FRONT & BACK
SKIRTS
Cut 2

side seam

fold

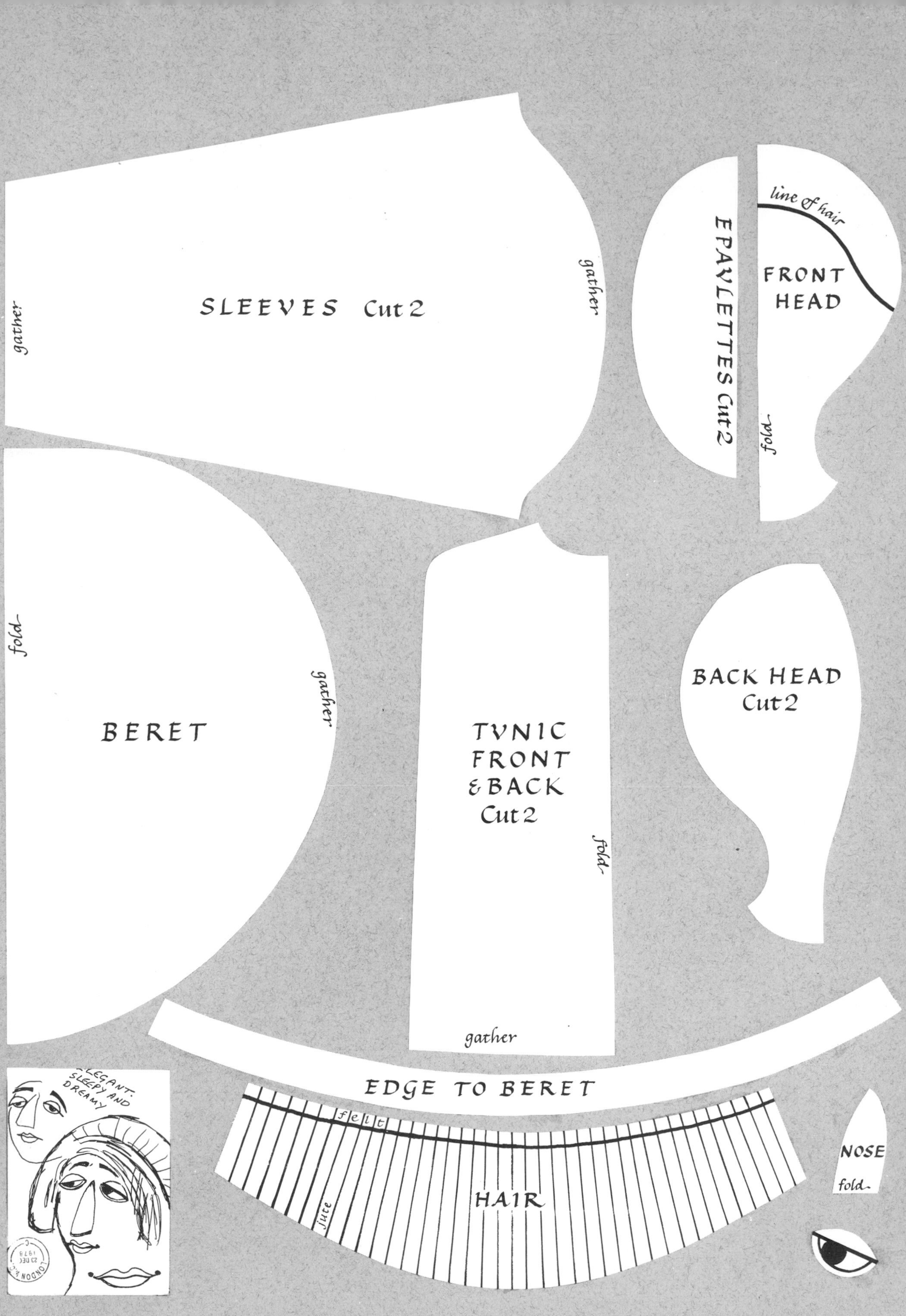

SLEEVES Cut 2

gather

gather

gather

fold

BERET

gather

TVNIC
FRONT
&BACK
Cut 2

fold

gather

EPAVLETTES Cut 2

line of hair

FRONT
HEAD

fold

BACK HEAD
Cut 2

EDGE TO BERET

felt

jute

HAIR

NOSE

fold

LEGANT:
SLEEPY AND
DREAMY

LONDON
23 DEC
1973

KNEE BANDS
Cut 2

A
SASH TIE
A
fold

A

A SASH BOW

sew A's to B

B

Depth of TOP LAYER

NECK FRILL

gather to neckline

SASH

WRIST FRILLS Cut 2

gather

MEZZETINO.

Correct proportions of basic figure

WATTEAU
MELANCHOLIC
LYRIC.

YELLOW HAIR.

LONGER BODY

SEQUINS.
PINKS.

USE (18)
DULL YELLOW
AND PEACH
SILK.

REDS.
BISCUIT

CARRY
GUITAR.
(BREAK)

Get character not just pretty

Possibly MANDOLIN with ribbon streamers.

Jewels.

CURVE
ARMS

fold-centre back

CLOAK
¼ scale

gather

SASH
ENDS

fold

CLOAK COLLAR
¼ scale

gather

SASH
ENDS

fold

TRIVELLINO
Conjectural

110

TRIVELLINO

Origins and Development

It is very difficult to obtain secure evidence on this character. It is possible that this was the name given to Arlequin during the early formative years of the companies. Certainly the information available suggests that his role was identical to that of Arlequin, or that he was one and the same person. A very great interpreter of the part who gained enormous popularity in Paris was Doménique Locatelli (1613-1671), but it is known that Locatelli played Arlequin as well. In one early eighteenth-century scenario the list of characters includes both Trivellino and Arlequin. Also, in an anonymous painting of the Italian players 'on stage' in France, both Arlequin and Trivellino are included together with Molière – and Trivellino is wearing a costume almost identical to the costume worn by Arlequin. Even more confusing, Arlequin sometimes wore a disguise covered in triangles, suns, moons and spangles – and this dress was usually associated with Trivellino. In the collection, this is the one figure where complete freedom of choice was used in the characterisation and the design of the costume.

Role

Accompanying Arlequin and playing games at the expense of the lovers, the Doctor, Pantalone or some other character. Like Arlequin he helped to keep the story-line together, or at other times to muddle it up.

Character

Mischievous and teasing, like Arlequin.

The Mask

The same as worn by Arlequin, but when wearing the spangled costume he may have discarded it.

Costume

Trivellino wore either the early version of Arlequin's dress (there is a print of Locatelli in this guise, unnamed) or an elaborate costume decorated with suns, moons and spangles, similar to those worn for the court masques, operas and ballets. A sort of fancy-dress at times strongly influenced by Greek and Roman fashion, ornament and decoration, the latter is used for this collection.

Movement

Quick, nimble and full of acrobatic feats.

Speech, Voice and Other Skills

No information is available on speech and voice but we do know that he possessed all the skills of Arlequin – particularly as an acrobat and tumbler. Vincentini, a famous Trivellino, could turn a somersault holding a glass of water or wine in his hand without spilling a drop. He would frequently leap from the stage into the auditorium, climbing out of the boxes and frightening the life out of the ladies.

Materials

Imagination can be used in the design and making of the costume for this character so long as it is based on masque costume of the time and decorated with moons, suns and spangles. Various forms of embroidery should be incorporated.

Cotton: natural coloured (head, nose, body)
  brown and orange narrow striped (smock)
  rough pale yellow (hat)
  striped brown and white (stockings)
  pink (cheeks)
Silk: brown (arms)
  beige (shoes)
  gold (shoes and knee rosettes, kneebands)
Lurex: gold (upper legs, suns)
  blue (moons)
Lace: white (sleeves) 6mm
  off-white (neck frill)
Various spangles and pearls: (smock decoration)
Various gold, blue and silver cords and braid: (smock decoration)
Braid: brown Russian (shoes, neckline)
Felt: white (eyes, moons)
  yellow (suns, neckline, basis for hair)
Jute: beige (hair)
Four gold buttons: (knee and shoe rosettes)
Dye: black (face features, suns and moons)
  red (suns)
  blue (moons, eyes)
Collection of different yellow, brown, white and pink feathers: (hat)
Card: (hat)
Padding

Making

Basic Figure: Assemble and sew all front and all back sections together. Sew completed front body to completed back body, turn right side out and pad. From the gold silk, make up 12mm-wide kneebands and sew them to the legs, covering the joins of upper legs to stockings. In the same material make up two rosettes, each centred with a gold button, and sew to the outside seams of the legs. Edge the top of the shoes with the brown Russian braid, adding similar rosettes, each centred with a gold button, to the fronts.

Assemble, make up and pad the arms and sew them firmly to the edge of the shoulders, completing the basic figure.

The Smock: Only the commencement of the decoration of the smock is shown on the patterns (the front and back, the yokes, and the sleeves). When finished it should look very rich with the addition of appliqué, painting, spangles, pearls and embroidery. Some of this ornament – the suns and the moons – can be applied *before* the smock is assembled. The remaining decoration – spangles and pearls, the bands around the hem and the sleeves, and the lace edges to the sleeves etc. – is added after assembly but before the smock is placed on the figure.

To make up, gather the tops of both the front body and the back body respectively to the front and back yokes. Now line the yokes in the same material. Oversew the shoulder seams together only as far along the neck edge as will allow the smock to be placed over the head of the figure with ease.

Lie the joined front and back body flat on a table and centre the tops of the sleeves to the shoulder lines of the body. Now sew the sleeves to the body parts. Next sew up the side seams of the smock right through including the sleeves. Hem the sleeves and skirt and finish decorating.

Place on the figure, sew up the shoulder seams that were left open and sew the neck edge to the neckline of the body. The smock is now complete save for the trimming of the neck.

Neckline: Trim with a deep frill of the off-white lace, terminating at the neck edge with a narrow band of yellow felt and a band of the brown Russian braid.

Hat: Make up the hat as described on p. 6, but omit the card stiffening for the brim. With a sewing machine sew ever-decreasing circles, 6mm apart, from the outside edge of the brim to the inner circumference. Then attach the brim to the crown.

Make up a fine display of feathers and glue them to the centre front of the crown. Lastly, lightly catch the back and front of the brim up to the crown with the back placed higher than the front. Do *not* sew or glue the hat to the head until the hair and the nose have been completed.

Head: Make up the sections for the hair, using the same process as with the other figures, looping the jute tightly together to the narrow strips of felt and glueing. Then cut the bottom edges of the jute and unravel. Now stick the fringe high to the forehead. Test the positioning of the hat, and stick first the underlayer and then, 6mm above, the top layer of hair to the sides and back of the head. Finally trim the fringe and length of hair.

Make up the nose, pad with soft cottonwool and sew in position.

The hat can now be firmly fixed to the head.

Position the eyes of white felt, and glue. Next, paint the pupils blue. The rest of the features should show Trivellino's naughtiness. The mouth, eyebrows and eyelids are all painted in black. The circular pink cheeks are cut from firmly-woven cotton and glued to the sides of the face very close to the eyes.

Accessories: Give him a small sprig of country flowers to hold in his hand.

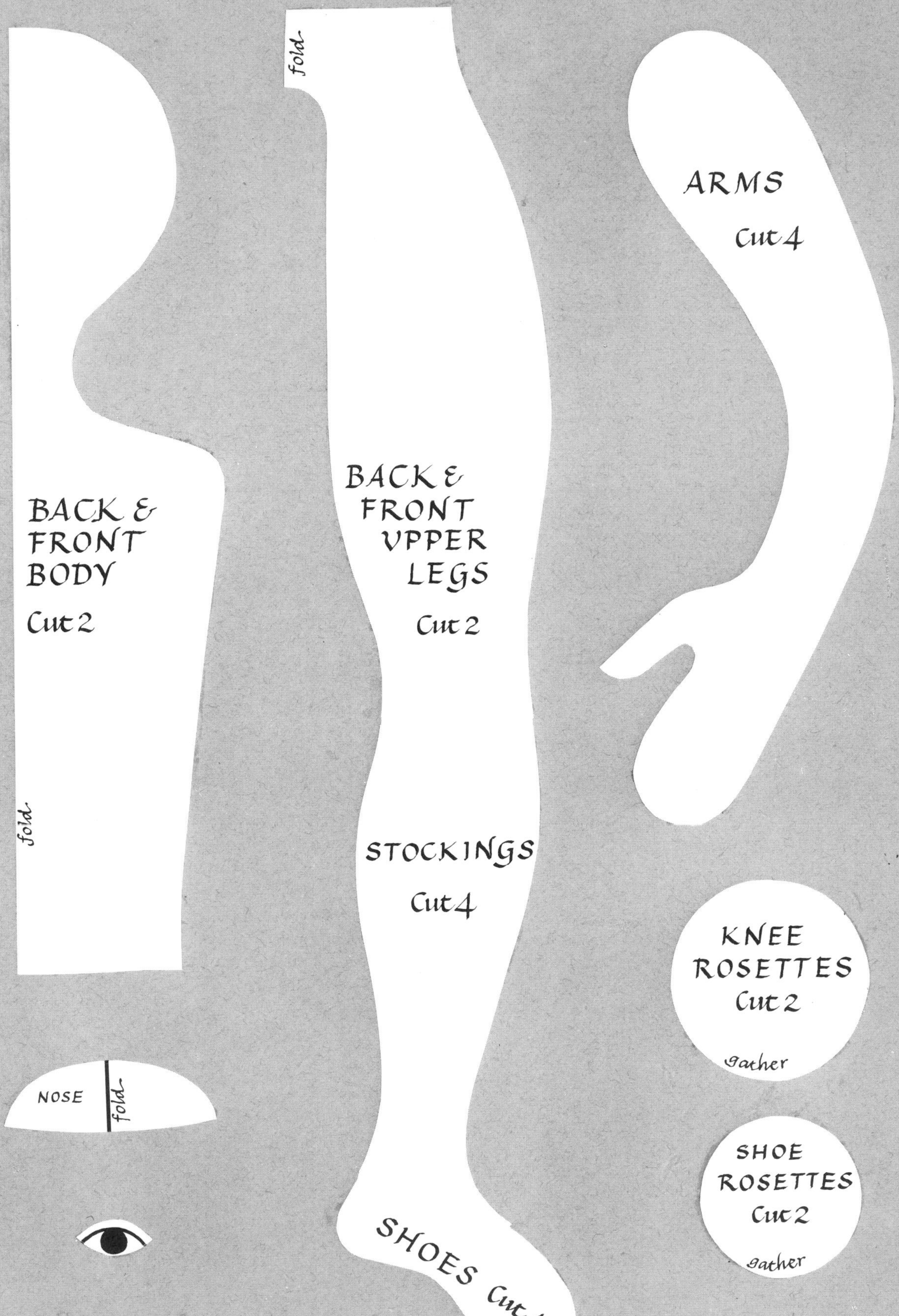

BACK &
FRONT
BODY

Cut 2

fold

fold

BACK &
FRONT
VPPER
LEGS

Cut 2

STOCKINGS

Cut 4

SHOES Cut 4

NOSE

fold

ARMS

Cut 4

KNEE
ROSETTES
Cut 2

gather

SHOE
ROSETTES
Cut 2

gather

armhole edge

side seam

side seam

SMOCK SLEEVES
Cut 2

1 FRINGE

FELT
JUTE
FRIZZED OUT

2

3

TWO LAYERS
TO HELP GIVE
BULK TO BACK
OF HEAD.

WIG.

SUNS
MOONS
SPANGLES — STARS
SEED PEARLS
SEQUINS.

gather to yoke

side seams

SMOCK BACK & FRONT
Cut 2

fold

fold

BACK YOKE TO
SMOCK Cut 2

fold

FRONT YOKE TO
SMOCK Cut 2

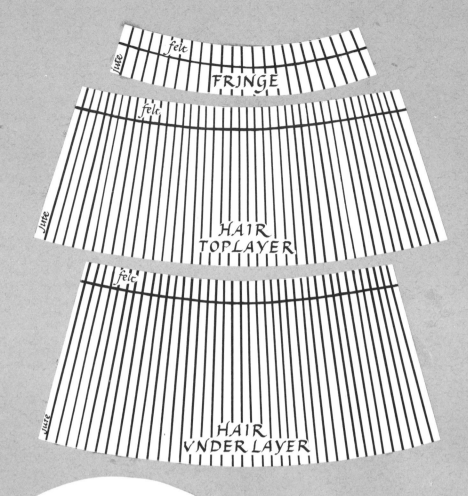

FRINGE

HAIR
TOP LAYER

HAIR
UNDER LAYER

BRIM TO HAT Cut 2

TOP of HAT

SIDES OF CROWN TO HAT

LOUIS XIV
Very freely based on the King wearing his robes of State

116

LOUIS XIV

Louis XIV was included in the collection of soft sculpture figures because of his great personal interest in the arts and his patronage of the Italian players. He was born in 1638 and succeeded to the throne in 1643 with Cardinal Mazarin as regent until 1661, when he officially became King, ruling his kingdom 'like a Roman emperor' (Voltaire) until his death in 1715. Including the time spent under Mazarin, he influenced French life for over seventy years, and exercised a despotic rule over his court, leaving them little or no time to involve themselves with the affairs of state.

He created an aura about himself with such assurance that even as a young man in his twenties he could appear in ballets dressed in elaborate masque costume as 'The Sun King'. Under his supreme control and kingship, France knew the most brilliant artistic and intellectual period in her history.

In 1655 Louis founded the Academy of Painting and Sculpture; he established the Academy of France in Rome in 1666, for the purpose of training French artists in classical techniques, and the Academy of Architecture in 1671. He encouraged the great Gobelins factory for the making of tapestries, furnishings and furniture for his royal palaces and public buildings. Few of the arts escaped his influence, as he became interested in town planning, architecture, painting, sculpture, the applied arts, music, literature, the design of gardens, fashion, etiquette and behaviour, ceremony, and all aspects of the theatre.

The court under his rule was the centre of national life in France. Splendour and magnificence reigned and his style of life affected the whole of Europe long after his death.

Costume

To interpret all the splendour of the Roi Soleil or 'Sun King' in his robes of State is not possible as translated into the medium of soft sculpture for a seated figure, as the great blue mantle of State would conceal most of his ornate dress.

In making the figure, therefore, the extravagant costume can only be expressed in essence, using 'artistic licence' and altering the cut of the mantle to reveal most of his suit of clothes. So his over-mantle is divided into two. The left side is covered by a mantle of blue scattered with golden fleurs-de-lis, edged with ermine and lined with cloth of gold, and from his right shoulder falls another cream gold drape or mantle, decorated around its border with blue embroidery and gold studs.

Thus revealed, he wears a heavily gold-braided doublet, with skirts in blue and gold. The old-fashioned late-sixteenth-century slops cover the upper parts of his breeches, which are of brocade like his sleeves. The sleeves join the shoulders covered by epaulettes. Elaborate bows, ties and ornament embellish the shoes, kneebands and belt.

The wig is in the height of fashion and his gold broad-brimmed hat is elaborately filled with white and blue feathers.

The deep lace-trimmed falling collar and upstanding cuffs are also very typical of the period. Over the shoulder-length ermine cape to his mantle he wears the collar of State.

Materials

Rich materials are essential for this figure. The colours should predominantly be in blue, gold and white. The use of rich braidings and ornamentation cannot be overdone.

Cotton: white (head, nose, collar, handkerchief)
    natural colour (hands)
    pink (lower lip)
Silk: pale blue (body, epaulettes, shoe rosettes, slops foundation)
    deep blue (skirts)
    deep cream (knees) 30mm fringe
    dark green shot with gold (stockings)
    blue raw silk (left mantle, shoulder cape lining, slops)
    pale cream gold (right mantle)
    blue embroidery (right mantle)
    white (shoes)
Lurex: gold (left mantle lining)
    gold, silver and blue patterned (arms, upper legs, knee-bands and rosettes)
Cloth of gold: (hat, waist rosette)
Turkey towelling: fine white (left mantle, shoulder cape)
Felt: yellow (hat)
    black (eyebrows, ermine tails)
    grey (eyelids)
    brown (foundation for collar of State, foundation for wig)
    white (eyes)
Lace: deep white (collar, cuffs)
    narrow white (handkerchief) 6mm
Ribbon: white (neckline) 12mm
    yellow (wrists, body, epaulettes) 12mm
    cream (right mantle)
    blue velvet (hat) 12mm
    wide blue and gold brocaded (panes to slops) 25mm to 35mm
    fancy white (shoes) 20mm
    fancy silver (knee rosettes) 20mm
Braid: white Russian (shoes)
    variety of gold braids (body, skirts, hat, left mantle, belt, epaulettes)
    gold fleurs-de-lis (hat)
Cord: gold (fleurs-de-lis)
Gold buttons: a handsome collection (body, knee, rosettes, shoes, belt)
Gold studs: (both mantles, collar of State)
Gold brooch: fine, small (finger ring)
Gold ornaments: from card or metal, including fleurs-de-lis, two letter *Hs* and a Maltese cross (collar of State)
Feathers: as fine a collection as possible, white and blue, including marabou, osprey and swan if possible (hat)
Jute: brown (wig)
Dye: black (face features)
Card: (hat)
Padding

Making

Basic Figure: Add a 45mm band composed of a variety of gold braids, with gold buttons set at regular intervals, down the centre front of the body. Assemble and sew all front and all back sections together.

Sew completed front body to completed back body, turn right side out and pad. Cover the side seams of the body with yellow ribbon. Add a double band of the cream silk fringe to the join of the legs to stockings, and cover these edges with 12mm bands of the patterned Lurex to form the kneebands.

Finish off on the outside seams of either leg with rosettes of the same material. The rosettes are centred with a gold button, backed with a double bow of fancy silver ribbon.

Edge the top of the shoes with the white Russian braid, adding pale blue rosettes centred with a gold button, backed with a double bow of fancy white ribbon, to the fronts.

Assemble, make up and pad the arms, adding and easing the darted lace cuffs to the wrists and covering the joins with bands of the yellow ribbon. Do *not* sew the arms to the body.

Slops: Make up the foundation in the blue silk. Then make up the slops proper in the blue raw silk. Following the pattern, add to the top edge of the slops proper lengths of the wide blue and the gold brocaded ribbon (the panes).

Now join the lower edges (marked X) to the lower edges of the slops. Evenly gather the top edge of the slops proper to the top edge of the foundation. Repeat the same process at the lower edge. Then place on the figure and ease and sew the waistline of the finished slops to the waistline of the body.

Skirts: Make up in the deep blue silk and line with the same material. Decorate the surface with bands of gold braid down the sides and around the hem. Sew the waist edge of the finished skirts to the waistline of the body.

Belt: The waistline is finished off with a 12mm belt of heavy gold braid complete with a gold rosette and a handsome gold button or buckle positioned at the centre front.

Arms and Epaulettes: Now sew the arms firmly to the edge of the shoulders. Cover the shoulders with epaulettes of pale blue silk lined with the same material and richly banded all round with the yellow ribbon followed by gold braid.

Blue Mantle (Left): With the gold cord couched to the blue raw silk, ornament the entire surface with fleurs-de-lis (50mm deep and each finished off with a gold stud positioned centrally 20mm up). Line the mantle with the gold Lurex. Add a 30mm band of the white Turkey towelling all round the edge both inside and out, save for the neckline. Glue little pieces of black felt at regular intervals around the outside band to simulate ermine tails. Around the inner edge of the Turkey towelling on the blue side, finish off with a narrow band of gold braid. Place the finished mantle to the left side of the figure, high at the neck edge, with centre front to centre front and centre back to centre back, and sew in position around the neck.

Pale Gold Mantle (Right): Dart and then hem all round, adding a band of cream ribbon, set in, down the sides and around the lower hem. Decorate this band with alternate gold studs and little embroidered blue stars set at regular intervals all round. Gather the top of the mantle to about 75mm and sew it centrally to the right side of the figure under the epaulette.

Shoulder Cape: Line the white Turkey towelling with the blue raw silk. Ornament the towelling side all over with little pieces of black felt to simulate ermine tails. Place the cape on the figure, centre front to centre front, and sew it firmly around the neckline, making sure that it covers the neck edge of the blue mantle. Then over-sew the centre back edges together. Depending on the thickness of the Turkey towelling, you may need to adapt the pattern to fit.

Collar: Dart and make up the collar in fine white cotton, lining it with the same material, and edge all round (save the neckline) with deep lace, mitring the six corners. Fold the two

front edges to the front (see pattern) and, placing it high to the throat of the figure, sew the collar in position. Cover this join with a band of white cotton ribbon, adding a bow of the same ribbon to the centre front.

Wig: Cut the foundation from brown felt (two side pieces and back) and make up as described on p. 5. To make the fringe, take a narrow band of felt and glue loops of jute, tightly packed together, to it. Cut the lower edges of the loops and unravel to form the fringe.

Glue the completed back piece to the back of the head and the completed side pieces to the sides, just overlapping the back section. Lastly, glue the fringe to the forehead. Make sure, when positioning, that the top edges of the wig will be covered by the hat.

Depending on how much jute has been used in making the wig, the size of the inner circumference of the hat may need to be made larger.

Hat: Make up the hat as described on p. 6, with the outside of the brim and the crown in cloth of gold and the inside of the brim in yellow felt. Edge the brim on the gold side with the blue velvet ribbon, 6mm deep when finished, and the top edge of the crown with gold braid. Now turn up the front of the brim and attach it to the crown.

Feathers fill the inside of the brim. First glue a length of white marabou all round the base of the crown. Then between the upturned centre of the brim and the crown glue a fine cockade in the shape of a pair of wings, fashioned out of white osprey feathers and centred with a burst of dyed deep blue swan feathers. Finally make up a fleur-de-lis in layers of firm gold braid and add this high to the back of the centre front of the brim. Do not fix the hat to the head.

Head: Make up the nose, pad with soft cottonwool and sew in position. The hat can now be sewn or glued to the head.

Glue to the face the black felt eyebrows and the white felt eyes with the upper eyelids in grey felt. All the features are painted in black, save for the lower lip which should be cut from a piece of deep pink cotton. Commence by painting in the mouth features followed by the chin, then the eyes, and lastly the lines beneath the eyes.

Collar of State: First test the foundation pattern to see that it sits neatly around the shoulder cape (adapt if necessary) and make up in the brown felt. Now use your imagination – and what is at your disposal – for the decoration, which should be very rich and handsome. Embellish the entire collar, starting at the centre front, with golden fleurs-de-lis. The central fleur-de-lis should be supported on either side with the letter *H*. From its base suspend a white and gold Maltese cross. Lastly, cover the remaining brown felt foundation with gold ornament. Parts of a French gold card birthday-cake frill, decorated with fleurs-de-lis, may be used for most of the decoration, including gold studs. Now place the collar firmly on the figure, securing it with a little glue at either shoulder point.

Handkerchief: Make up in fine white cotton, hem all round and edge with a narrow band of lace. Place and sew it to the right hand.

Finger Ring: Select a small and beautiful ornament and sew it, in an appropriate position, to the left hand.

The collection is now complete, but to give King Louis his right as the essence of the baroque, let the blue mantle be looped up and held in his left hand.

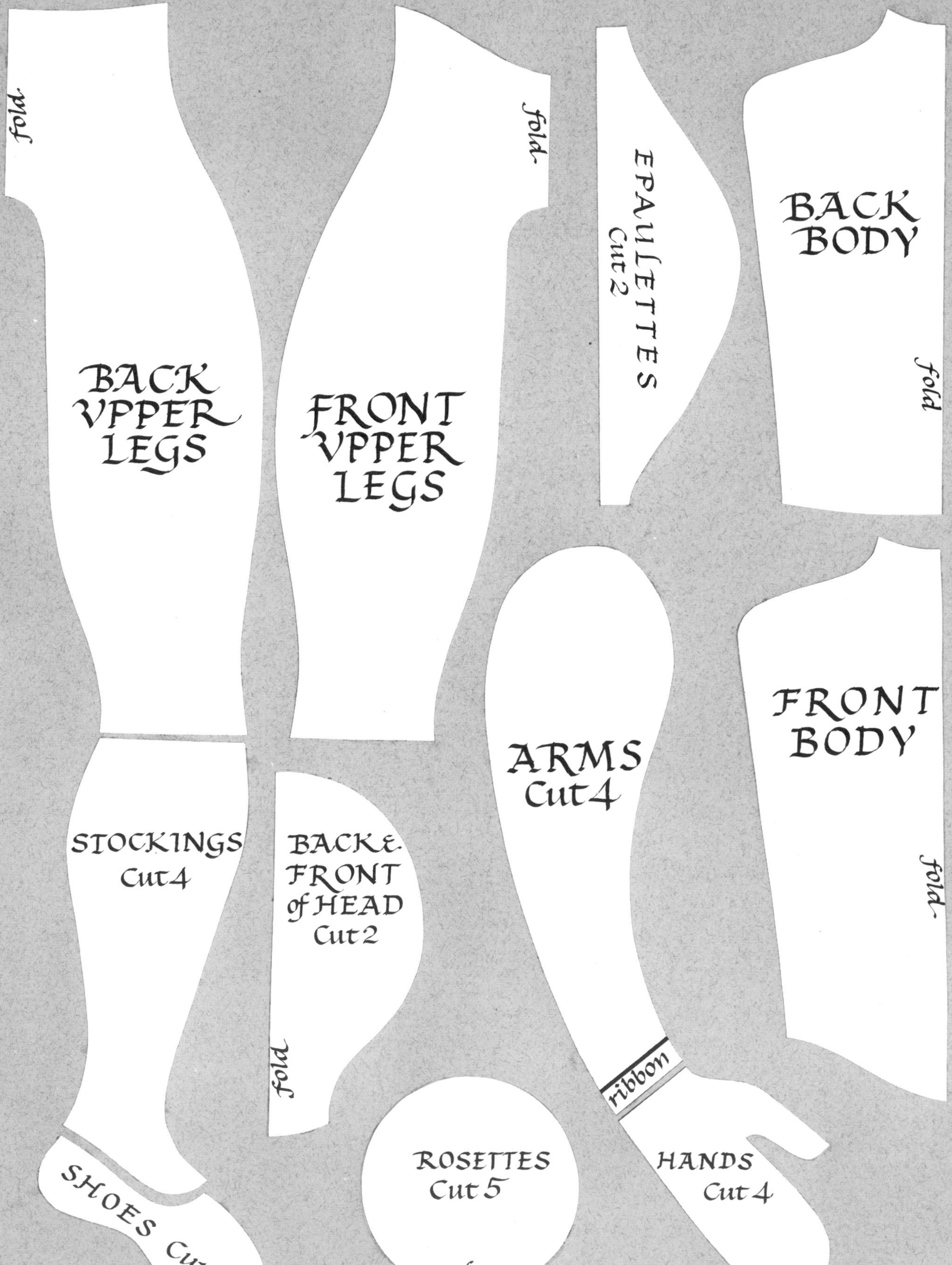

BACK UPPER LEGS

fold

FRONT UPPER LEGS

fold

EPAULETTES
Cut 2

BACK BODY

fold

ARMS
Cut 4

FRONT BODY

fold

STOCKINGS
Cut 4

BACK &
FRONT
of HEAD
Cut 2

fold

SHOES Cut 4

ROSETTES
Cut 5

gather

ribbon

HANDS
Cut 4

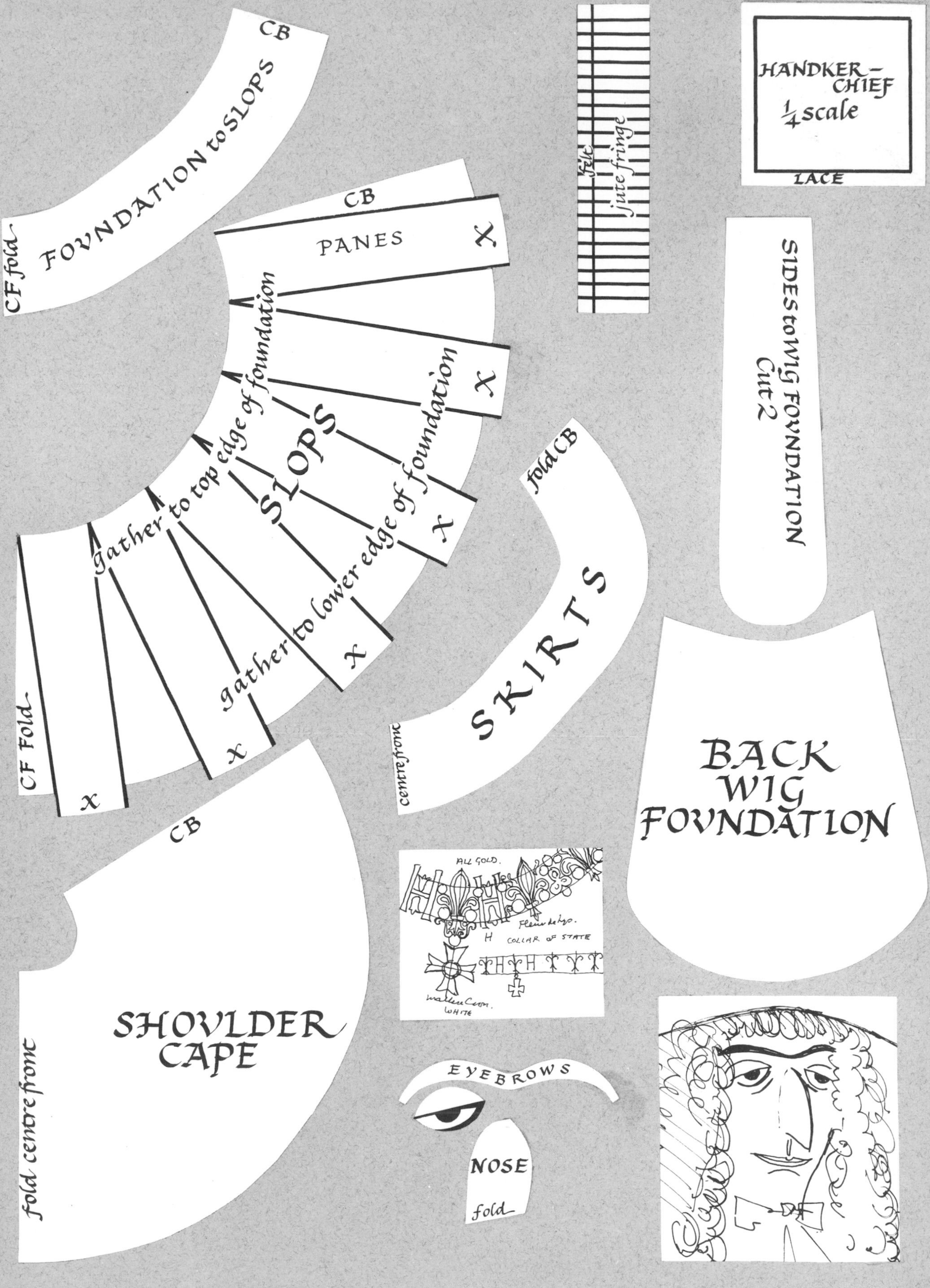

CB

FOUNDATION to SLOPS

CF fold

CB

PANES

X

Gather to top edge of foundation

SLOPS

Gather to lower edge of foundation

X

X

CF Fold

X

X

X

X

X

fold CB

SKIRTS

centre front

CB

SHOULDER
CAPE

fold centre front

Felt
jute fringe

HANDKER-
CHIEF
¼ scale

LACE

SIDES to WIG FOUNDATION
Cut 2

BACK
WIG
FOUNDATION

ALL GOLD.

Fleur de lys.
H COLLAR OF STATE

Maltese Cross.
WHITE

EYEBROWS

NOSE

fold

BRIM to HAT

TOP of HAT

Cut 2

CVFFS Cut 2

DART

FOUNDATION for COLLAR of STATE FRONT & BACK Cut 2

SIDES of CROWN to HAT

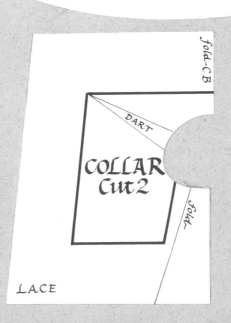

centre front

centre back

BLVE MANTLE Left

$\frac{1}{8}$ scale

fold-CB

DART

COLLAR Cut 2

fold

LACE

dart and gather

GOLD MANTLE Right

$\frac{1}{8}$ scale